Jonathan and Sarah:
An Uncommon Union

A Novel Based on the Family
of Jonathan and Sarah Edwards
(The Stockbridge Years, 1750-1758)

by
Edna Gerstner
(Author of *Idelette*)

Soli Deo Gloria Publications
...for instruction in righteousness...

Soli Deo Gloria Publications
P.O. Box 451, Morgan, PA 15064
(412) 221-1901/FAX 221-1902

*

Jonathan and Sarah: An Uncommon Union
is © 1995 by Edna Gerstner and Soli Deo Gloria.
Printed in the United States of America.
All rights reserved.

*

ISBN 1-57358-011-2

*

Second Printing 1996

To yet another Jonathan
—ours.

Thank You:

Jennifer Coffin
Kim Kistler
Mary Semach

Introduction

This delightful novel, written many years ago, is an insightful and poignant story detailing a portion of the life of Jonathan and Sarah Edwards during their missionary years in Stockbridge, Massachussetts. We are charmed from the beginning by such an intimate and captivating glimpse into the private family life of one of history's most significant figures. Much of the information was taken from the actual diaries of the Edwards family to enhance the accuracy of this moving account of their life together. Through this story we gain a fuller picture of the character of the great Edwards, seen as a devoted and loving family man.

Sarah Pierrepont, just seventeen when she married Jonathan Edwards, was known as a gentle, pious, and intelligent beauty. But it was her "endearing graces" and unique spiritual temperament that drew Edwards to her. Sarah walked with God in what the author describes as a mystical, quiet communion, seeking Him with an "unweaned resignation to the Divine Will."

Edwards, known for his keen intellect, expert logic, and analytical precision, was twenty-three when his life with Sarah began. Theirs was a marriage of mutual respect and admiration—"a rare and beautiful relationship." Sarah promoted the wise building of her home by respecting her husband's nearly thirteen hours a day of study time and managing her eight children through the running of a disciplined household.

Jonathan Edwards is described as a husband and father whose care and oversight of his family was thoroughly spiritual. He took seriously anything that troubled his children, and would save the evening hours to be spent in prayer and close fellowship with his family. Primarily concerned for the condition of their souls, Edwards taught each of his children to earnestly seek salvation, "to have God our friend, and to be united to Christ."

The sweetness of Jonathan and Sarah's relationship is engaging reading as the story spans the years of Edwards' most prolific writing, and includes some of the most dramatic family changes. Jonathan and Sarah, each in their own way, were "given to God," and the legacy they left is remarkable. Their love for one another was manifestly a reflection of the deep and profound love that each had for Christ and their unfailing commitment to come together in marriage to serve the One who had first loved them.

The depth and selflessness of their love stirs and encourages us even today. You will enjoy learning more of the Edwards family life and this "uncommon union."

Kim Kistler
Pittsburgh, PA
June 1995

"The Puritans were too honest to dilute
the vinegar of life."

—Harriet Beecher Stowe

OUR INDIANS

"My wife and children are well-pleased with our present situation. They like the place far better than they expected. Here, at present, we live in peace; which has of long time been an unusual thing with us. The Indians seem much pleased with my family, especially my wife. They are generally more sober and serious than they used to be. Beside the Stockbridge Indians, here are above sixty of the Six Nations, who live here for the sake of instruction."

—Jonathan Edwards

1

Mary Edwards held Dulcie's reins lightly. She watched her husband ride away to see about the damaged fence. All the Edwards family, her in-laws, rode well. They had that quality of horsemanship by which, when mounted, they became one with the horse. With her, riding was merely a means of locomotion. She was always timid astride and much preferred, whenever possible, to use the chaise. Even today, alone in the carriage with the gentle horse, she felt uneasy.

"I will only be a moment," her husband said, "and it is much cooler for you waiting here in the chaise under the trees by the riverbank."

The mare tossed her head. It had been a hot drive and she was thirsty. She eyed her rider and tentatively gave a tug to inch closer to the river. Feeling no tightening of the reins she ventured a step. As usual, Mary gave the horse her head and the thirsty animal bent down to drink.

The delicacy of cool water upon her parched tongue tantalized the horse into going deeper. Forgetful for the moment of the rider with so slack a rein, she pranced into the stream pulling the fragile chaise over the bank into the river. Mary was flung free and fell, striking her head against a rock jutting out of the shallow water.

The horse panicked and ran, trying to free herself from the broken chaise that dragged along behind her. No trace remained in the stream of the exact spot into which her rider had fallen; and, although the horse and riderless carriage were quickly found, it was an hour before Jonathan Edwards, Jr. found his wife's body. She drowned in water so shallow that, had she not been knocked unconscious by the fall, she could easily have waded to safety.

Alone that night in the four-poster bed his wife Mary had brought with her from her home in Hadley, Massachusetts, the bereaved man lay awake tearless and still stunned. He was unable to bear thinking of the present, of Mary who no longer lay beside him, of his four motherless children. The canopy above his head wove in and out moved by the breeze from the open window. As he stared at it open-eyed, he found himself seeking escape from the present, like a hurt child, by crawling back to the days of security of his childhood.

No longer was he Jonathan Edwards, Jr., pastor of the New Haven congregation. He was a child in his parents' home in Stockbridge, Massachusetts. The canopy was the one over his parents' bed. And he had crept in with them.

Little Jonathan Edwards was full of imagination. His older brother Timothy was the active one, the doer. But the weakness of the younger boy's eyes made him more dependent upon an imaginary world in which to play; and at night this world came awake. The stories he had heard from his American Indian playmates peopled his room with frightening shapes, and he would cover his eyes and run across the hall. His mother, Sarah, always moved over, and in the warm hollow which her body had made in the big bed he would fall quickly to sleep hearing the breeze ruffle the flowered canopy above him.

His father slept heavily, but in the morning he was always the first awake. It had been his arms the drowsy child had felt carrying him back to the room he shared with Timothy.

How wonderful it would be to live as bravely as Timothy. He never seemed to mind awakening in the shadowy night. He did not people the corners with frightening images. Timothy was practical. On a sleepless night he would lie awake and utilize his time planning for the day ahead.

Jonathan was slower than his brother in many ways. He was the last of all the children to learn to read. He was six and still could not read, for his eyes would tear and water if he tried to follow the print. His curious mind was forced instead to learn through his ears. He listened while the others read to him, and when they were too busy to oblige he ran to the wigwams of the Indians among whom his father labored, and sat and listened to their lore. Whenever possible he would unlatch the gate and run fleetfooted through the British settlement to the Indian village.

His brothers and sisters said that he was more Indian than English. They pointed out that when he walked, he toed in like an Indian. And it was a known fact that he never cried except within. The Indians, who changed the names of their children as they grew to describe their personality variations, had named this youg boy of six No-Cry Eagle.

No-Cry Eagle learned well with his sensitive ears. He listened, and while he helped the Housatonnucks, the people who lived by the waters, mend their butterfly-shaped fish nets he acquired a wisdom not found in books. He learned from them the language of the falling waters and the growing grass.

2

Jonathan sat outside on the cold ground beside his friend, Fleetfoot, and watched as the Indian whittled a baby's rattle for his little brother, Turkeylegs, who hung in his cradle board in the tree. The little papoose's eyes remained fixed on his brother, anticipating in his baby way that what Fleetfoot was doing was in some way connected with him.

The big squaw, their mother, stayed within the wigwam. It always seemed strange to Jonathan how big the Indian squaws grew. The braves remained tight and muscular, the maidens were like the willow trees that fringed the river, but soon they seemed to settle into this soft fatness which all the squaws possessed. Jonathan did not find it unattractive. Unlike the pioneer white women, many of whom grew gaunt, with the years they became fat, soft, comfortable pillows.

Both boys were silent while Fleetfoot worked. During most of the time Jonathan spent with his Indian friends words were few. Here he found none of the constant chatter which at times upset him in his household of brothers and sisters. Satisfied with his final flick of the knife, Fleetfoot took the gourd rattle to give to his young brother. Turkeylegs cooed and gooed his enthusiastic thanks.

"Naughty boy!" rebuked the squaw.

Jonathan was not surprised. He knew this was a part of the Indian training. As the child grew he would learn not to show enthusiasm, or any expression on his face. He too would achieve the so-called "wooden face" of the Indian, which the tribe so much admired and which was so perplexing to one who did not understand the Indian.

Now the baby's transparent joy in the new toy was indulged and, because of his age, evoked only a slight rebuke. In time he would learn. Big brother Fleetfoot never smiled. He would look at Jonathan with no expression in his eyes, yet Jonathan knew that between them there was a strong bond of affection. The Indian smiled inside. Jonathan had learned to look past the exterior and was able to read happiness, anger, and other subtler emotions in the face of his friend.

Now, with babysitting chores finished, the two boys raced to their ponies and tore off into the forest. Turkeylegs wailed at this treacherous desertion. Mother took him down and hung him near her so he could watch her cook. He settled immediately into his contented staring, this time at the big woman around whom his whole world revolved.

3

The two bodies of American Indians forming the mission parish of Jonathan Edwards were as different as two ethnic groups could possibly be. The ones in the majority, living in Stockbridge, were of the Housatonnuck tribe. They were referred to by the colonists as the Stockbridge Indians. They were peaceful, isolationist people, living quietly by the waters, as their name implied. But shortly before the arrival of Jonathan Edwards at this outpost, an influx of Mohawks and Oneidas had settled in this fertile valley. These newer members were a part of the larger Iroquois nation, fierce fighters and much feared by all, red man as well as white. Under the astute leadership of the great chief Hiawatha in 1750, five of the tribes had united to form this strong confederacy of the Iroquois. These tribes were the Mohawks, the Oneidas, the Onondagas, the Senecas, and the Cayugas. Francis Parkman called these warriors the "Romans of the New World."

Two of the family of the Iroquois, the Mohawks and the Oneidas, migrated to Stockbridge, and by 1750 about ninety Mohawks and Oneidas were in residence. The Oneida stone was set up in a crotch of the tree by the river. They were now again a stationary people, and considered themselves invincible when this stone was at rest.

It was no small feat to move this stone, cylindrical in shape and weighing about one hundred pounds. It was regarded with great awe by the tribe. The very name of the tribe was derived from this stone, for Oneida means "the upright stone." Whenever the tribe migrated the stone went with them. A stout man could carry it for forty or fifty rods without resting, and this is how it was tenderly moved by hand.

There were altogether three divisions of the Oneidas—the Wolf, the Bear and the Turtle. But in all, as is the case with many American Indians, the children belonged to the family of the mother and not the father, and were counted with them. When a marriage did not work, it was father who left the home to go back to his own mother.

The Oneidas were governed by their adoration of the good spirit and their fear of the evil. They were extremely superstitious. In one settlement, when a man drowned in their good fishing waters, they refused to fish there again. It was only when an Englishman from Fort Stanwyx, understanding their fears, sprinkled powder on the water and told them he had purified it that they reopened their fish nets. In this case the deceitful act of the Englishman was meant in all kindness, but because they were so subject to fear they were frequently prey to unscrupulous men who betrayed their childishness, their superstitions, and their trust.

These were some of "Our Indians" of whom missionary Jonathan Edwards spoke affectionately. The names on the roll were misleading. Very few gave any intimation of Indian origin. For it was completely natural for the American Indian to add a new name at the time of Christian baptism. They selected these names to suit their personalities. On the rolls were an Isaac, a Solomon, a Jacob, a Hannah, a John, a Mary, a Rebecca, a Benjamin, a Josiah, and a Peter.

Not only did the converts prefer Bible names, but they had a very high veneration for the English language, feeling in a misguided way that this was truly the language of God. The first convert in the Stockbridge mission under missionary John Sargeant, after his baptism, asked also that his marriage be made a Christian one, insisting on the use of the English language in his marriage service.

Often their new names were embellished with an adjective. Peter, for example, was always called "Good Peter." He was a faithful member of the church. His wife, however, refused to join with him and, in accordance with the tribal customs, the children belonged to the squaw. Thus, though Good Peter was a pillar in the church, his squaw and all his children served their pagan gods.

Only in their surnames were the colorful backgrounds maintained. The interpreter for Jonathan Edwards at the service for the Housatonnucks was

John. His last name, which he continued to use, was Wonwanonpequuunnonnt.

The same church building was used for all services by the settlers and the American Indians. The building was located on the green. It had three doors—one on each end and one on the south side—pews against the walls, and two aisles. It was, as were all the churches of the period, of two stories: a ground floor and a gallery.

Rather than having a bell toll the hour of the service, the people were called together by a large conch shell from the East Indies, a gift from the people of Boston. Both white and red man contributed to the salary of the conch shell blower, who also served as the janitor.

The key man in the church service was the interpreter. Mr. Edwards's delivery varied little from that of his Northampton days. Although there was no bell rope on which to fix his eyes, he gazed steadily in that direction. It was an oft-quoted joke that he had gazed so steadfastly at the bell rope in Northampton that when it fell it was said that he had "preached off the bell rope."

Mr. Edwards was very deliberate in his speech. His interpreter, however, was of a more lively personality. While Mr. Edwards made his logical predictions, his interpreter sprinkled daisies about his chain of arguments. It was as well that the missionary's knowledge of the native language was meager. It was difficult at times for little Jonathan, who understood both, to remain sober when he sat listening to the two versions.

Pastor Edwards kept his sermons exceedingly simple for the primitive parishioners. It amazed his erudite friends how well his great mind could adapt to the situation. He who found the thoughts of Locke no hurdle could speak to the heart and mind of the child.

While the mission outpost of Stockbridge remained exposed to complete annihilation from the enemy without, daily duties were discharged with extreme and tender care, being given to those of the same race who were the friends within.

The conch shell was never silent.

4

Jonathan Edwards, the preacher, spoke very slowly in simple English, addressing the strange congregation assembled before him in the meeting house.

The room was sparsely filled with a handful of Mohawks. Twice each Sunday, in addition to two sermons in English for the settlers, the missionary preacher spoke to his Indian parish. These sermons to the Mohawks and to the Housatonnucks were relayed through an interpreter. For although the missionary could speak haltingly in the language of the American Indian, he never felt he had reached the perfection necessary for the delivery of a sermon in the foreign tongue.

This morning he spoke on the evils of drink. Drink was their "darling vice," he stated. "It was a great log across the path which the traveler can't climb nor go round."

His congregation watched him impassively. The preacher could read no response, affirmative or negative, in their faces, for the Indian mind is not an easy one to read. But his son Jonathan, this morning the only white face among the red, knew with an instinct, Indian-trained, that the old men especially were agreeing with their missionary.

He sensed that while his father, with his usual logical thoroughness, pointed out that the destiny of the habitual drunkard was hellfire, this future aspect concerned them less than the practical points he made relative to the dangers of drink in this present life.

At the close of the sermon, the grave-faced Indians wrapped their blankets about themselves and clustered about Mr. Edwards. They seized this opportunity while the man was ministering to their souls to point out the many grievances their temporal bodies were undergoing. The Mohawks respected this new missionary. He listened to them with an impartiality they valued, and already they had seen many changes for the better in their Stockbridge situation, most of which they had despaired of ever achieving.

Whenever they faltered for a word, it was to young Jonathan both sides turned. The lad never lacked for the exact idiom with which to express himself in either language. And sometimes the Mohawks used young Jonathan not only as an interpreter but as a mediator. They stood in awe of Mr. Edwards, but the son Jonathan had slept in their long houses on the thick corn husk mats with their own sons. He had watched their young braves play lacrosse. He was an expert with their young sons at stick in the snow.

Today, walking home holding his young son's small hand in his own, the father thanked the boy for the splendid assistance he had given him. Young Jonathan flushed with pleasure. He loved these private times with his father.

"The American Indian, my son, believes unlike us in one common parent, that mankind was made instead of one clay. We differ only because of the baking process. Even as they place their clay pottery into a hot oven, they attribute this act to the Great Spirit in the art of creation.

"With the first batch of clay, the legend goes, he tried too hard, he left the ingredients in the oven too long, and the people came out black. Anxious not to repeat his error, the next lump the great Spirit removed too soon and out emerged us—the palefaces, the half-baked ones. But the final segment was perfect, for having profited by his past mistakes in workmanship, the last result was his finest creation, the people of the warm red earth, the American Indian.

"The American Indian is a proud race. It is a lesson we English never seem to learn. We are inherently convinced of our own superiority and then it astounds us to find others possessing even in their legends this same feeling of being the chosen people.

"We dress for dinner in the wilderness in insular arrogance. It were much better, Jonathan, if like you we could seek out the wigwams of the Housatonnucks and the long houses of the Mohawk and eat round corn cakes with maple syrup while the wind makes music from the hanging gourds and the turtle shells dangle from the rafters.

"You are an American, my son. Use your heritage. You will be wilderness-bred. Although I want you to feel at home with your own, in the drawing rooms of culture, I am grateful to God that you are also one with these good people of the red earth. It is a gift I do not possess. Even when I try, I remain a part of me aloof and alien. Never turn your back, my son, on the wigwams of your friends 'who live by the waters.' "

And while his father continued to talk to him of the American Indian, his young son listened. "These people must have a written language. Only then can the worlds of culture, but especially the Bible, be completely open to them. Many translators could do this, but the first step, the most difficult step toward the evangelization in a large scale of the American Indian, is the writing of an American Indian grammar."

"I shall write one for them, Father."

"You may, my son. In the providence of God you may be the one best fitted for the task."

It was the way of Mr. Edwards to take the remarks of his solemn son seriously. And on the walk home that day the seed was sown for a major work, *The Language of the Mouhhekaneow Indians,* by Jonathan Edwards, Jr.

5

The language of the Stockbridge Indians, the Mouhhekaneow, was a very difficult one. In many ways it was more analogous to the Hebrew than to the English. Jonathan Edwards, although a Hebrew scholar, never felt proficient enough in the new medium to preach in it.

But his young son dreamed in the language. He spoke little English outside his own home and was a little master of his adopted tongue. This speech of the Stockbridge Indians was the one used by the majority of the Indians in North America. It had differences, for example, from the dialect used by the Shawnee Indians, but not enough to make communication impossible. For example, the word for "bear" was "mquoh" in the one and "mauquah" in the other.

However, the language of the Iroquois, of the five nations, some of whom had moved to Stockbridge and with whom Jonathan Edwards also labored, was vastly different. This language, for example, unlike the other, abounded in labials. Jonathan counted for his father in the language of his friends of the village: "Ngwittch, Neasah, Noghhoh, Nauwoh." Then to illustrate for his father the difference he had noticed by studying the speech of the boarding-school students, who were for the most part Mohawks, he tried this stranger tongue: "Usket, Tegenneh, Ohs, Kialeh, Wisk."

"Do you know the Lord's Prayer in the Mohican?" asked his father, who was proud to be able to be in the role of a student, his young son the professor.

The lad intoned the words in the language of the Six Nations: "Soungwauneha caurounkyawga tehsetaroan sauhsoneyousta esa sawane ou...."

His father joined him as they both said the prayer in the language of the Stockbridge Indians, the Housatonnucks: "Noghnun, ne spuamuck cieon, taugh mauweh wheh wtukoseauk neanne annuwoieon...." There was no similarity. Jonathan Edwards had to preach to both groups each Sabbath, and the time necessary to master both languages could best be used in other pursuits, he ultimately concluded. Hence the decision to use the means of an interpreter.

But for secular communications he attempted to learn the language and use it. Not infrequently young Jonathan would be called in to help. From the boy the scholar learned that the Housatonnuck or Stockbridge Indians had no way of expressing a word absolutely. It always belonged to someone. A relationship had to be established. For example, no Indians could understand the word "father" in the absolute. It must always be "my father," "your father," or "his father." It had to belong to someone.

A hatchet which was lost, or which no one could claim to possess, could sometimes be referred to by itself.

Also from his bright young son he learned that the scholars of the day erred, however, when they thought the Housatonnucks had no abstract terms. The Stockbridge Indians did have a concept of love, "unwhundowakon," or hatred, "seekeenundowukon."

While trying to increase one's vocabulary, one had to be extremely careful not to be misled in this search for new words. If, for example, one stretched out one's hand the Indian's answer would be "the hand"—knisk. If you pointed, however, to the Indian's hands it was always "unisk,"—his hand.

Jonathan Edwards faced the problem which has beset all translators, all pioneers in philology. He could have understood so well the frustrations met by the missionary to the Bantu people of Africa. Whenever this translator pointed to an object he received the same answer, "Bosai, bosai." Everything—sky, moon, earth, dog, woman, child—all were "Bosai." The angrier he became the more amused were his African friends. They thought he was being playful. It was much later he stumbled on the fact that he was not being teased by the Africans. They were consistently giving him the word for finger, for he was pointing with it. Unlike him, the Bantu did not know the gesture of pointing with a finger. The Bantu would thrust out his lip, his method of pointing.

Much of the delay in acquiring a new vocabulary Jonathan Edwards escaped because his young son knew not only the vocabulary but the customs of the people. They grew very close as they studied together. They discovered that the Housatonnucks had no adjectives, their verbs themselves flexibly adapting to this lack. They learned also that the language knew no gender. When they tried to speak English one would often find a brave referring to his spouse with "He is my wife." Knowing these differences made it easier to teach the American Indians the English speech, for one could point out these distinctions and alert the learner to them.

Father and son spent endless hours working together. No one appreciated more than his own father the uncanny aptitude of the young son, not only to be aware of basic differences but the parrot-like way he caught the dialect without any British accent intruding.

The effort was important. For in addition to the Shawnees, the Delawares of Pennsylvania, the Penobscots who lived on land bordering Nova Scotia, the Indians of St. Francis in Canada, the Chippewas who lived west of Lake Huron—all of these tribes could benefit by a systematization of the language of the Housatonnucks, the Stockbridge Indians. Even the language into which Mr. Elliot had translated the first Bible in the American Indian language was largely the same.

Jonathan Edwards himself wrote no definitive work on philology. But he sparked the mind of his son, and encouraged a drive which ended in a research work of clarity and distinction. At the moment, man and boy were content to whet their minds upon each other.

6

Jonathan Edwards's interest in the Stockbridge mission had begun with its conception. It had been started in 1734 in the town of Northampton, largely due to Colonel John Stoddard. This distinguished gentleman was the son of the minister of Northampton under whom Jonathan Edwards served as assistant pastor.

Colonel Stoddard was perhaps the best informed man on Indian affairs of anyone in his region. It was he who felt that settling in the Housatonnuck territory was wise, for these Stockbridge Indians were not yet under French and hence Roman Catholic influence.

Northampton had been the mother church to the new work. But in addition to his own parish interest in the project, Jonathan Edwards had become intimately involved in its infancy due to his deep friendship with that fiery, gentle missionary to the Indians, David Brainerd. Missionary Brainerd's own missionary outpost had been Kauunaumeck, eighteen miles north of Stockbridge.

For a time it seemed Jerusha, the gentlest of Jonathan Edwards's daughters, a true child of God, would marry this young man and spend her life

with him in the evangelization of the American
Indians. When all the devoted care the family ac-
corded was unable to stop the ravages of David
Brainerd's disease, and he died in their Northampton home at the age of thirty, his message of
parting to his betrothed had been, "If I thought I
should not see you, and be happy with you in another world, I could not bear to part with you. But
we shall spend a happy eternity together!" It was on
October 9, 1747 that David Brainerd died. His fi-
ancee, Jerusha Edwards, recorded her father in his
own hand in the family records, "died on a sabbath
day, February 14, 1748, about five o'clock in the
morning, aged 17." She outlived her David by only
five months.

Mr. Edwards devoted as a memorial to these two
he loved, and whose missionary work together
would never materialize, a biography which he
drew in detail from his own memory of the missionary. He wanted to preserve that soul aflame for
later generations to know even as he had been priv-
ileged to know it.

Now it appeared as if this work of authorship
alone were not sufficient. And when God led he
was especially happy for an opportunity to bring
God to the tribe which Missionary Brainerd had always called "my people." It was as if by becoming a
missionary to the American Indians he was extending the lives of the ones so dear to him.

But although both David Brainerd and Jonathan

Edwards were zealots for the evangelization of the red man, their approaches were totally different, even as their own personalities were opposites. David Brainerd went out to reach the people. He lived with the American Indians in his own wigwam, ate poor Indian fare, and spent many a night sleeping in the saddle. Throughout most of this time he suffered severe hemorrhages from his weakened lungs. His good friend Edwards too late persuaded the young man that it was a sin against the Almighty to burn out for God rather than to live out his life for Him. In the biography of the missionary, Jonathan Edwards recorded that the young man "had been more resolute to withstand temptation to such degrees of labor as injured his health." But his resolution had come too late to save his friend's emaciated body.

Jonathan Edwards never consciously sinned against his own body. He took every precaution to live out his life. He husbanded his health. He made himself cut wood for one half-hour a day for necessary exercise away from his desk. He rode for relaxation, but he made no arduous treks into the wilderness. The romantic approach of the firebrand was not his. He made himself available to those who came to him.

Rather than learn their language, he felt the American Indian should learn English, the tool of civilization. His argument was the futility of mastering a language which had not yet produced anything to read. He wrote frankly, "The Indian languages are extremely barbarous and barren, and very ill-fitted for communicating things moral and divine, or even things speculative and abstract. In short, they are wholly unfit for a people possessed of civilization, knowledge, and refinement."

But although he had no high regard for their speech, his respect for these people he held in common with the few of that day who could sense and appreciate the grandeur of the original American. David Brainerd loved the red man; Jonathan Edwards respected him.

He used his influence whenever possible in their behalf. When the Mohawks, restive because their grievances in Stockbridge were ignored, threatened to leave in revolt, it was he who wrote urging that work among this great nation, the Iroquois, be continued. And when he could not stop their final departure in disgust from Stockbridge, it was he who helped to choose a new missionary outpost at Onoquanga, near the head of the Susquehanna River, as an arm by which to keep them under the care of the church. And this time he helped see that the missionary appointed over them was a man who loved God and the red man.

Eloquently he wrote the commissioners in Boston on their behalf, "There are some here who have sometimes spoken contemptuously of them; but there are other persons in Stockbridge who have had as much opportunity to know what is the true state of these people as they. The Onohquaga Indians, who have been here, are properly not only of the Six Nations, but of the Five Nations, who are the original united tribes of the Iroquois. All, but one or two of them of the nation of the Oneintas; and they appear not to be looked upon as contemptible by the rest of the Five Nations, from what was openly said of them at a public council by the sachems of the Conneenchees, or proper Mohawks, who advised us to treat the Onohquagas with peculiar care and kindness, as excelling their own tribe in religion and virtue. We have found the testimony which they have of them to be true. They appear to be by far the best disposed Indians with which we have had any connection. They would be inclined to the utmost, to assist, encourage, and strengthen the hands of missionaries and instructors, would any be sent among them, and to do all they could to forward their success, among themselves and the other Indians round about."

Notwithstanding this regard, Jonathan Edwards had moments of despair. He wondered if he were making any headway with the Indian mind. He asked himself the questions: Could they learn? Did they want to learn? Was his own method at fault? It was his predecessor, Missionary John Sargeant, who had urged him not to make his own mistake of spending too much time trying to learn the difficult language of the Indians, and instead devote more effort to introduce him to the key language of English. But were they both right?

His work seemed sterile in contrast to how God had blessed the labor of Missionary Brainerd, as well as how dramatically! One of the favorite stories Edwards's own children loved to hear David Brainerd tell was of the remarkable awakening of a whole Indian village.

The missionary had slipped away at dawn that day before his friends were awake lest they stop him. He had clung to his saddle, weak from ill health, only to falter at the very outskirts of this pagan village, his destination. He had fallen from his saddle and crawled to bury his head against a hollow log to pray. As was his custom when alone in the woods he prayed aloud in anguished entreaty to God for souls, the souls of his "dear people."

The sachem of the tribe had almost stumbled over him. He and his braves hid in the bushes watching the anguish of the missionary. They did not like this troublemaker who stirred the people from their old ways of worship. They feared their evil spirits would turn their corn wormy and their hunting pastures barren if they listened to his strange talk. One brave, seizing the opportunity, set an arrow to his bow and aimed. Unaware of his onlookers, David Brainerd prayed on. As the arrow was about to be released, instead of firing the brave lowered his bow. Out of the hollow log crawling toward Brainerd, the brave sighted a deadly rattlesnake which had been disturbed from his slumbers by the noise of fervent prayer. It amused the Indian to let the snake do his work for him.

The braves watched the rattler raise its head to strike. The impassioned missionary prayed, swaying in ecstasy. Whether his gentle swaying soothed the snake like the snake charmer's flute, or whatever the cause, it seemed impossible for the snake to strike. Three times it rattled and reared, only to lower itself to the ground and slither away.

Never in their forest experience had they seen such a phenomenon. It was enough for them, enough to break down a door, a door on which the impassioned missionary had been pounding for years. Instead of killing David Brainerd, they tenderly carried him to their own wigwams and nursed him back to health. God used this natural means. God gave them a heart of flesh and the entire village professed to accept the wonderful words of life.

The ministry of Jonathan Edwards by contrast was never spectacular among the red man. He was sure, ultimately, that he was discharging his duties as he perceived the will of God. He felt his was the duty to sow the seed. It was God who decreed the increase. And if there were to be no repetition in this outpost of the great revival he had conducted in Northampton, it was the will of God.

But he searched, in his moments of discouragement, among the journals of David Brainerd to

see if there could be something in his life, some
lack of spark or spirit, that could be traced to a fault
in himself. This man, never a mystic himself,
never despised those whose own experience of God
seemed more ecstatic than his own. He had written
of David Brainerd and his transports that he was a
man also of "close reasoning and exacting judgment."

Jonathan Edwards's wife was a constant
reminder to him of the spiritual temperament of
David Brainerd. For Sarah had, since childhood,
been given to mystical transports. She seemed to
walk with God. By nature inclined to be analytical
and skeptical, he had wondered for a time if her
transports were related in some way to hysteria, and
he had bought medicines to calm her.

His friend and physician, Dr. Samuel Mather,
had once written to him regarding his wife, "I think
that my *fichtus emplastrum matricale* would be of
great service to her if applied to her navel and worn
there for some weeks or months together. It's an
admirable remedy in all diseases retaining to an
hysterical original, and I have seen surprising
effects from this application in Histrick [hysterical]
cases. I think it would be worth your while to send
to Boston for it, as I have none of it at present."

But in time he doubted their physical origin. He
forthwith encouraged her to examine these moments of ecstasy, hoping that by her writing an analytical account of her experiences, any part that was

not holy would become apparent to her. For from the beginning he never felt that she could be other than self-deceived. In the end he had to write of his wife, "Now if such things are enthusiasm, and the offspring of a distempered brain; let my brain be possessed evermore of that happy distemper!"

In the same way he dealt with the elations of David Brainerd. As he wrote the life story of his young friend, he wrote truthfully that the young man was given to melancholy. But the amazing fact was that Mr. Brainerd was able to recognize in himself the difference between "melancholy" and "godly sorrow." He was led to comment, "It is a rare thing indeed, that melancholy people are sensible of their own diseases."

Although he never felt transported to the skies, he loved too deeply, and admired too much, these two mystics in his own life to ever feel free to condemn the ecstasy. As for himself, without the use of wings, he continued to walk with God.

7

Stockbridge Village counted among its citizens many from illustrious families. Two in the Indian village were noted chieftains.

The first member to join the Stockbridge Church was Ebenezer Pooponah, an interpreter. The second who was admitted into membership was Captain Konkapot, a chieftain. At his baptism he wanted to have his name changed, as was the way with the Indian to denote a character change, and he selected the New Testament name John. His wife chose for her new name that of Mary. John and Mary Konkapot were loyal and dedicated Christians.

Mary was one of the first of the Indians in Stockbridge to fatally contract that new disease to the red man, an old plague of the whites, tuberculosis, and died from it on March 29, 1741. She witnessed to her faith jubilantly on her deathbed. It was said of her that she enjoyed "during her sickness a good hope, through grace, of a happy eternity." Her daughter, Catherine, died young and shortly thereafter. Once again a strong faith in God was notably manifest. It was said of her that her "hope raised her above the fears of death."

The two sons of Captain Konkapot lived to rear families. Jacob, inheriting leadership qualities from his father, often became the spokesman for his people, especially feeling it his duty to present the growing grievances of his race before the missionary pastor.

Abraham Konkapot, unfortunately, stepped from the path of his father, destroyed by yet another vicious death-dealing disease introduced by the white man. After having earned for himself the honor of being the select man of the village, he had been "drowned," the records go, "in intoxicating bowl."

On the membership rolls of the church there was the family of Lieutenant Umpachee, whose wife was a daughter of E-To-Wau-kaum, a distinguished chief who had visited England under the reign of Queen Anne. Both the Lieutenant and his wife had died before Jonathan Edwards took up his pastorate, but their children were members.

There was the family of Captain Ninham, the Quinney family, one of whose descendents married a Methodist clergyman, Amohawk, a missionary among the Oneidas and the Senecas. This young woman, upon the death of her missionary husband, married again, an equally illustrious man, who was instrumental in establishing the first American Indian newspaper among the Cherokee tribe.

And of course there was the Aupaumet family. Captain Hendricks Aupaumet dropped the Indian name, and later the descendants were known simply as the Hendrickses. Captain Hendricks never joined the church but did all he could to help the cause of missions. He was a man of integrity, which caused him to give credit to the church for this great blessing to his own people. There was found in him none of the ingratitude that flares in so many pagan lands where non-Christians grab the fruits of Christianity only to despise the Gospel roots.

Hendricks, as he was called, was a great name on the early American frontier. He was the shrewdest of the Indian fighters. He was a wise warrior and a great help to the Colonies. In the battle against the French commander, Baron Diewkau, the plan had been at first for the British to send a smaller force than they were opposing. Hendricks's vigorous opinion was, "If they are to fight, they are too few; if they are to be killed, they are too many."

His pre-battle speech, urging his own braves to do combat, was so eloquent that a soldier who understood nothing of what was said was so moved by the sight of the Indian figure mounted on a gun-carriage, eyes ablaze, dynamic gestures with voice inflections, that he told everyone everywhere that it was the most affecting speech he had ever heard!

When at this same battle the English had planned to divide into three parties and attack separately, Hendricks's advice, as was his manner, was pictorial. He took three sticks and placed them side by side, united into one clump. "Put them together and you cannot break them; take them one by one and you can break them easily." He effectively demonstrated his point.

Hendricks's father had been called "The Wolf." The son possessed much of the stealthy craft of that animal. He was staunchly loyal to the British, and his personal friendship with the minister of Indian affairs, Sir William Johnson, was augmented when that British gentleman selected Hendricks's own sister, Molly Brant, as his wife.

Though he never joined the Stockbridge church, he encouraged any who wished to join its communion. He sent his own son to the mission school.

Hendricks wrote in his own words the history of his race and some of the Mohawks' ethical customs. It was the practice of the head of the family to awaken the others tenderly with the following ritual:

> "My children, you must remember that it is by the goodness of the Great Good Spirit we are preserved through the night. My children, you must listen to my words. If you wish to see many good days and evenings you must love all men and be kind to all people. If you see any that are in distress, you must try to help them. Remember that you will also be in distress some time or other. Though you

should have but little cake, give him half of it, for you also are liable to hunger. If you will not assist or have compassion for the poor, you will displease the Good Spirit. You will be called 'Uh-wu-theet,' or hard-hearted, and nobody will have pity on you in the time of your distress, but will mock at you.

"My little children, if you see an aged man or woman on your way doing something, you must have pity on them and help them instantly. In so doing, you will make their hearts glad, and they will speak well of you. And you must not be hasty to speak when you hear people talking, nor allow yourself too much laughing.

"My children, you must be very kind to strangers. If you see a stranger or strangers come by the side of your fire-place, you must salute them, and take them by the hand, and be friendly to them; because you will be a stranger some time or other.

"My children, again listen. You must always speak nothing but the truth wherever you are; otherwise, when you should bring tidings of importance with the truth, they shall not regard what you say.

"My children, you must never steal anything from your fellow man, for remember this—you will not be pleased if some of your neighbors should take away your things by way of stealing; and you must also remember that the Great Good Spirit sees you. But if you will allow yourself to steal, you will hurt your name, and disgrace your parents and all relations; and you will be despised by all good people.

"My children, you must always avoid bad company. And above all you must never commit murder. If you commit murder, the Great Good Spirit will be angry with you, and your life will be in great danger; also the lives of your dear relations.

"My children, you must be very industrious. You must get up early in the morning to put on your clothes, moccasins, and tie your belt about you that you may be ready to do something. If you will be lazy, you will be always poor.

"And further, my children, when you are grown up you must not take a wife or husband without the consent of your parents and all relations. But if

you do contrary to this, perhaps you
will be joined to one who will bring
great darkness to you, and thereby you
will be unhappy.

"My children, at all times you must
obey your Sachem and Chiefs in all
good counsels they give; never speak
evil against them, for they have taken
much pains in promoting your happiness. And if you do not observe this,
you will be looked upon worse than
the beasts are."

Thus, related Captain Hendricks in his history, it
appeared his fathers had instructed their children
day after day. This custom had been handed down
from one generation to another.

The motive for a life of righteousness was
frankly utilitarian and practical. Honesty pays.
There was ingrained in their ethical ritual even a
touch of "Do unto others as you would have them
do unto you." But there was no trace of righteousness for the Creator's sake or the concept of love for
enemies.

Yet it was enough to make the Mohawks stand
tall ethically among the pagan nations, and to cause
the missionary who labored for their salvation to
say of them that "they excel their own tribe in religion and virtue."

8

The American Indian was not really red. His color was that of the rich brown earth. He early received the name "red" because of his habit of painting his body before going on the warpath. The Indian the settlers most feared was the painted Red Indian. Quickly, to avoid confusion, they adapted this description to distinguish the Indian of the North American continent from the brown Indian of India.

The Mohawks with whom Jonathan Edwards had done most of his work were a very proud race. They belonged to the Iroquois tribe whose men were skilled hunters and fishermen and warriors of renown. It was the Iroquois who were noted for their rites of torture. This suffering, which so shocked the civilized world, was exquisite to them for they felt it showed a man's true character to try it by fire. The women of the tribe would be present at these tests and would sing songs to encourage the prisoner who unflinchingly endured all the devious methods of torture the braves could devise.

During times of peace the Mohawk men spent their hours making bows and arrows and spears or harpoons for their fishing industry. Or they would

sit and weave their lightly twined fences, another
method by which they trapped fish. Some would
spend their time carving their dreaded war clubs.
They built their long houses. Unlike the
Housatonnucks, who slept in wigwams, the Mohawks lived in long dormitories. These they made
by driving two rows of poles into the ground in
zigzag lines, ten or twelve feet apart. They bent
these poles and tied them together at the top, with
other poles fastened across them. The roof was
made of bark strapped to these cover poles with an
open space left at the top to accommodate the
smoke from the open fires. The long house would
have only two entries, a door at either end. Usually
the only doorway would be a hanging curtain made
from animal skins.

Down the center of this dormitory ran a wide
hall. This served as the communal kitchen, with
many families sharing the same fire. The only privacy the unit had was a small room, often only six
by nine feet, divided from the next usually by a
leather curtain. Beds were usually made of thick
corn husks which served as mattresses. These were
spread on the floor and made comfortable by a top-
ping of rich skins and furs.

Occupants in each long house were usually related, with grandfathers, uncles, and aunts each oc-
cupying an allotted unit. Every ten to fifteen years
the clan moved depending upon the scarcity of fish
or game. Sometimes, however, the move was or-

dered because it was much simpler to move to another location and build another house than clean the old one.

A Mohican village would consist of two or more long houses. For reasons of safety, the Mohawk would build his home on a hill where the view was best. But always the villages were by the river, for the Indian depended upon the fish for fresh food. The river was also the superhighway of the day, the quickest and easiest way to travel. The Iroquois built sturdy elm-bark canoes, but abandoned their own method of ship building when they discovered the better maneuverability of the light and beautiful birch canoes of the northern tribes. Since portage was a major factor with them, their own sturdier canoes were not preferred, being too heavy to compete with the lighter canoe. When in winter the river froze, they traveled instead by snowshoe, making sleds to carry their goods.

The men cleared the trees and brush, but after that their house chores were ended. The women were the farmers and planters. They made holes in the ground with a planting stick and dropped in the seed of the three sisters—corn, bean and squash. To avoid weeding, the wise women planted beans with the corn, and the twining beans would choke out the weeds.

The women were also the food gatherers. It was they who gathered the delicious wild rice from the meadows, the wild onions and the garlic. For refrigeration they dug holes in the cool earth, lining each one with bark or fur, covering their garners for sparser days. Their long houses were always dangling with the ears of corn or the squash that hung from the ceiling.

Jonathan Edwards, Jr. felt at home in the stockade surrounded by a bevy of sisters. His American Indian friends spent all their early youth with their mothers. In fact, the little papoose never left her side. While mother worked he would be hung from his cradle on the limb of a tree. His eyes would focus on her gardening or scraping the skins to make the deerskin coat which one day would be his. The Indian gave the little one complete security by never separating the baby from the mother. They knew that when the time came their boys would make braver warriors because they had not known fear when too young to understand it.

The first work a young boy did was to help his mother. Until he was old enough to fish and hunt with the braves, he helped gather in the fruits and nuts that abounded in the forests. He was especially diligent in the season of the wild strawberry, for this picking time ended with a strawberry festival, a thanksgiving period of fun and dancing for a good ingathering.

It was the squaw who disciplined the young. Spanking was not their way of punishment. Rather, the method the Indian mother found most effective was picking the young one up by the heels and dipping him into the river. Many a stranger observed that Indian boys were better behaved in cool weather, their morals somewhat affected by the temperature of the water.

The women also made the clothes for the family. The Mohawk women loved beautiful skirts. Their own garb of skirt and vest was made of the softest of the deerskin. Their necklaces were made from shells adorned with animal teeth. Their braves, in summer, wore only a deerskin breechcloth. In cold weather they wore long leather leggings and long tunics that looked like shirts. Both sexes wore soft deerskin moccasins on their feet. These they made by soaking the skins in water and then scraping the hide with a sharp stone until all the hair had been removed. The final touch was to rub the skins together, working them between the hands until they were as pliable as silk.

The beliefs of the Mohawks were very simple. Entreat the good spirits, especially the Great Spirit. Pacify the evil spirits. One could almost say, however, that they worshipped the great god corn. This was their very staff of life. They lived mainly on a mush made from the corn which the women pounded on a stone, and to which, when available, meat and vegetables were added. They ate a round cake also made from corn, like a pancake. Sometimes this corn was mixed with maple syrup and dried. One could exist on these for a steady diet, for they contained in them all the minerals and vitamins essential for survival.

In gratitude, most of their festivals dealt with corn. In the spring there was the Corn Planting Festival. After the long winter came the Festival of the Green Corn. In fall, at the time of the harvest, was the Harvest Festival, with strange music being made by the shaking of rattles made from gourds and turtle shells and Indian drums. Once again corn appeared with the wearing of corn husk masks used to frighten away the bad spirits.

Many a Mohawk stayed away when he heard the conch shell call to Sabbath worship only because he feared that, if he went, his corn would become wormy and his family would starve.

The early colonist understood this practical strain in the religion of the Indian. A favorite house motto in their own cabins was "Give us this day our daily bread." Anything would do: corn or, in the worst of times, turnips.

9

The Sabbath meal at the Edwards table was very simple. Turnips were the one staple food that the family could always count on having. Times were hard; gone were the days when father's salary was among the highest paid to a minister of God. Now what money came in was derived from three sources: the Society for the Propagation of the Gospel in London, the Boston Commissioners, and the two small local congregations. And, as is so often the case when the responsibility is shared, no one source was dependable.

Jonathan Edwards's own private fortune was tied up in the beautiful home in Northampton for which no buyers were forthcoming. The children helped to augment the unsteady income. The girls embroidered and made lovely laces and attractive fans to sell on the Boston market. The boys helped farm the steady crop of turnips. Father economized on the reams of paper he needed for his scholarly writings. Every scrap of paper was treasured and utilized. Often some profound sermon thoughts or outlines of his latest new work, *The Freedom of the Will*, would be written on the back of the latest doctor's prescription. There were always plenty of

these, for although the family of eleven was re-
duced to eight in Stockbridge, someone always
seemed to be requiring medication. Grocery lists ran
side by side with thoughts of God; "our daily bread"
paralleled the "hallowed be Thy name."

But if it was turnips on the platter, the talk
around the Edwards table was gourmet. The
younger children, like all well-behaved colonial little ones, said nothing unless addressed. "Speak
not!" was the table etiquette demanded of them.
"Children were to be seen and not heard," but the
older young people were granted the privilege of
speech as adults, and the vivacious girls, Esther,
Lucy, and Susannah, tossed the ball of conversation
spicily about. Father, whose stomach was delicate,
was usually absent. He preferred to eat his restricted
diet alone as an aid to his digestion. He joined the
family only on special occasions—although he always said the grace before the meal with his family,
and rejoined them at its close for the giving of
thanks.

Today he tarried with them. They discussed,
first, the most recent of the frequent Indian complaints. The Hollis Boarding School, which was
supported by money from Britain by the philanthropic Mr. Hollis, was the subject during this particular meal. The Mohawks at the worship service
had complained that their sons had found lumps of
grain filling in their meals, salt meat and porridge,
and there was too little of that diluted food.

The Boarding School situation was a scandal, and it was an inherited problem. When Jonathan Edwards was assigned the new position at Stockbridge, he was to minister to the English population and also, especially, the Housatonuck Indians. The Housatonnucks' language was Mouhhekaneow. Missionary John Sargeant, Edwards's predecessor, had been concerned about the work; and his advice to the new incumbent was that less time be spent learning the difficult language of the Indian and more time spent teaching the American Indian English. Jonathan Edwards, on investigating the school situation, was concerned seeing that the American Indians had been taught to read English but with no comprehension. They read words accurately but with no sense of their meaning. He was fired with a vision to start a method of teaching reading according to his own ideas, avoiding all the pitfalls of the present teaching of English. His logical mind balked at parrot learning. He felt more time should be spent helping the children understand thoughts.

"One of the great defects, as I humbly conceive," he wrote to Sir Williams who was in charge of Indian affairs, "is this, that children are habituated to learning without understanding."

If this new method of teaching were employed, his argument went, "This will be a rational way of teaching. Assisting the child's reason enables him to see the use, and end, and result of reading, at the same time that he takes pains from day to day to read. It is the way also to accustom the child from its infancy to think and reflect, and beget in it an early taste for knowledge, and a regular increasing appetite for it."

He wanted also to have a great finale at examination time, a fiesta, making this examination a public one, inviting the trustees, all in town connected with Indian affairs, neighboring ministers, gentlemen and ladies, and, above all, the chieftains. Prizes would be awarded. Refreshments would be served. This would be an American intellectual gymkhana. This, Mr. Edwards felt, would appeal to the Indian mind. It would be "pleasing and animating" to the tribes of Indians.

Both Mr. Sargeant and Mr. Edwards felt that the best way to teach the English language was to have the student live with it, constantly exposed to it by having each placed in a family where correctly spoken English was used. Either this, or the student should be placed in an English-speaking boarding school.

Rev. Isaac Hollis, a minister living near London, was inspired with a zeal to do something along these lines and underwrote the expense of twelve Indian students. A boarding school was started, but when Mr. Edwards arrived at his post he found this good work in the hands of a misfit. Unable to secure a teacher proficient both in English and, especially, the difficult language which the American

Indian boys spoke, the school unfortunately had hired the only man available for the job at the time, a Captain Martin Kellogg.

The new schoolteacher, Mr. Kellogg, originally a farmer, then a soldier, was about sixty years of age. He was lame physically, but, it appeared, also mentally crippled and totally unequipped for the job. He and his sister, Mrs. Ashley, the wife of Captain Ashley, in their youth had been taken prisoner by the Iroquois and with the agility of young children had picked up the speech of their captors. Mrs. Ashley used this ability now and served as the official interpreter for the English at Stockbridge. She was very efficient, admired and loved by all. Through her, her brother, because of his skill in the Iroquois language, was placed temporarily in the post of the first schoolmaster of the Hollis Boarding School. What seemed a good idea at the time backfired. Loath to lose the money the Hollis foundation brought to him, he refused to relinquish his job.

Thus what started in all good faith was now bogged down due to the greed of one man. There was another difficulty at the Hollis Boarding School which also stemmed from good roots. Mr. Sargeant and, later, Mr. Edwards in turn urged the Mohawks who lived about forty miles west of Albany along the Mohawk River to send their youth to the Boarding School. They accepted this offer for education and also, at the invitation of the Stockbridge

Indians, many Mohawks moved to settle there. Some of the big chiefs came also.

Neither missionary had anticipated what now developed. The Housatonnuck boys would not go to the same school as the Mohawks. They were afraid of them. In the end the Boarding School which had been started to serve the Housatonnucks was abandoned almost totally to the Mohawk youth.

Now Missionary Edwards also, in addition to having to add a sermon in the language of the Mohawk Indians, had to have two catechism classes for each group. He firmly believed in individual contact of teacher and pupil and utilized this direct teaching method. He had to satisfy this need. But as a result he had three catechetical groups—English, Housatonnucks, and Mohawk—running concurrently.

The Housatonnuck Indian children were not neglected academically, however. They sent their children to a day school run by a Mr. Timothy Woodbridge. They had the benefit of a man of true excellence, one of the earliest settlers of Stockbridge, selected as the teacher because of his piety to live in this outpost town so that by his influence he could help the Indians around him.

Mr. Edwards was very happy to have a man of this quality in his day school. He described him as a "man of very good abilities, of a manly, honest, and generous disposition, and as having, by his upright

conduct and agreeable manners, secured the affection and confidence of the Indians."

Nobody, however, was happy about Captain
Kellogg. His sister, a good woman, was embarrassed
but unable to budge him. He spent most of the
school time plowing, putting the Mohawk boys to
work on his farm for him. He had fallen into a soft
spot and exploited it to the full. It was a very embar-
rassing situation for Mr. Edwards to inherit. It was
not easy to have to inform Mr. Hollis, the earnest
British clergyman, that most of the money he had
sent to evangelize the Indian had gone into the
down with which a retired soldier was feathering
his nest. Something had to be done. Until the
source of income was cut off, Mr. Martin Kellogg
would remain the schoolmaster of the Hollis
Boarding School.

The Mohawks were shrewd. They hated the situation. They constantly threatened to leave
Stockbridge in protest. And they were always at the
door of the resident missionary with their justified
complaints. What would he do for their sons who
were being fed the meagerest of fare both in their
minds and their stomachs, and at the same time
worked in the fields like slaves?

Mr. Edwards's intellectual friends were distressed to learn that Stockbridge was promising to
be no haven for a man of letters. He had left
Northampton only to walk headlong into a mesh
of problems which entangled him and kept him

from greater endeavors. They despaired, for they had hoped that this giant of an intellect, this "whale confined to a small puddle," would find time in Stockbridge to produce works that his situation in Northampton had rendered impossible.

They knew too well the character of Jonathan Edwards. He would do the task at hand. If the Lord placed him in a situation where he must legislate on lumps of porridge, he would do it fairly and ungrudgingly.

What a tremendous wave of relief was felt when Mr. Edwards wrote to his friend in Scotland, Mr. Erskine, that not only had he begun his philosophic work on *The Freedom of the Will*, all the while harassed by his problems at the outpost, but had finished the treatise in the space of four and a half months. "A careful and strict Inquiry into the Modern prevailing Notions of that Freedom of the Will, which is supposed to be essential to Moral Agency, Virtue and Vice, Reward and Punishment, Praise and Blame" was ready for the press.

His biographer and friend, Samuel Hopkins, could not help but write, "So far as I am aware, no similar example, of power and rapidity united, is to be found in the annals of mental effort."

How was this feat accomplished? Partly by the affection and respect in which his family held him. His harassments came from without, not from within his family circle. His study time was not interrupted, and he usually managed the time-consuming chores, in this case, of a frontier household. The children saved their troubles, the ones Mother could not meet, to share with their father during the evening hours, which he always saved for his family.

But mainly this treatise was written because of the amazing way Mr. Edwards had learned to live with life. The worries of this life, these "frowns from heaven," were faced but never brooded about. He could leave them to lose himself in the skies at will. He had learned the secret of the Christian life, "Thou will keep him in perfect peace, whose mind is stayed on Thee."

10

The problem of the Hollis Boarding School was always a running complaint. But over today's Sabbath meal they discussed a new and grave matter. There were rumbles of trouble, the Mohawks were warring with the Hurons, and all the families of Stockbridge lived too close to the massacre of Deerfield to take any Indian war casually.

The frontier lived constantly under the shadow of the French and Indian wars which had broken out much earlier under the reign of William III. The rivalry of the English and French in Europe had extended across the seas. Both, desirous of territorial power in the new world, used, for the first time, a new and deadly weapon—the American Indian. This debased method of warfare was devilishly successful. Savages were incited to attack the settlers, and civilized nations sat back and watched barbarism set loose.

"You and the French," said one of the Indians to an Englishman, "are like the two edges of a pair of shears, and we are the cloth which is cut to pieces between them." Another Indian, seeing the French clan all on one side of the Ohio and the English all on the other side, inquired, puzzled, "Where then are the lands of the Indians?"

Between the French whom they called their "fathers," and the English, whom they called their "brothers," they were being "shared" out of the whole country.

The first blow had been struck by the Indians at Cocheco, now named Dover, New Hampshire. The officer in command of the English, Major Waldron, had thirteen years previously tricked and imprisoned some four hundred Indians. He had invited the red men to engage in a supposedly sham battle, and then had his soldiers surround and capture them. Half of these captives had been sold as slaves, and the other half he had executed in Boston.

Now the eighty-year-old Major Waldron was surrounded by the American Indians who had not forgotten. Friendly squaws who had been living with the English betrayed them and opened the stalwart doors at midnight. These homes had been built strongly to resist attack, but with the heavy doors of the garrisons open the English were helpless. Major Waldron was no coward, and he seized his sword and did his best to halt the attack, but he was struck down and stunned with a hatchet blow. Then he was dragged into his own hall and placed in a chair which was set upon the table. The Indians mocked him, their former magistrate, and jeered at him, "Judge Indians now! Judge Indians now!"

Not only was his past treachery uppermost in their minds, but they came fresh with recent grievances. They knew he had defrauded them when they sold him beaver skins, and that while he weighed them he cheated them by placing his fist in the scale to tip it in his favor. Now those in his debt gashed him with their knives saying, "I cross out my account." Others hacked his fingers from his hand saying, "Now will your fist weigh a pound?" Finally, as he was fainting from loss of blood, they placed the dying man in such a position that he fell upon his own sword. Their vengeance was terrible; twenty-three were killed, and twenty-nine residents of Cocheco were taken prisoner.

The frontier was ablaze. Retribution, at first limited to the perpetrators of past crimes, went afield. Innocents suffered for deeds of which they were totally unaware. In Stockbridge the cry of caution was always "Remember Deerfield."

Deerfield, this palisaded village on the Connecticut, was a small outpost with a garrison of twenty soldiers. One blizzardy night, a party of two hundred French and one hundred and forty-two Indians on snowshoes reached its vicinity, and the heavy drifted snow enabled them to quickly scale the town over the pickets. The sentries had abandoned their posts due to the intense cold. The terrible warhoop was the first notice of alarm the dazed villagers received. All the homes except one were put to the torch. Miraculously it and the village church escaped the fire.

All the inhabitants were tomahawked or taken

captives. The Reverend John Williams, later re-deeemed in an exchange of prisoners, gave his own eyewitness report of the tragedy. He had been aroused by the sound of axes and hatchets against his doors and windows. He put his pistol to the heart of the first Indian who jumped in but it mis-fired, and Mr. Williams was immediately seized and bound. He and his family were allowed to clothe themselves, and then they, together with the other captives, began a pitiless death march to Canada in icy snow knee-deep. His wife, having only recently given birth to a child, was too feeble for the trail. When she fell exhausted in the snow she was tomahawked.

The Indians had a march to make; they could not tarry for stragglers. There was no pity for the weak; only the strong survived the march. One hundred and twelve captors started on their march to Canada. Nineteen of his fellow prisoners were killed on the way and two starved to death. Yet, through God's grace, the minister relates, "The savages were moved by God to pity our children. They carried some of them on their backs."

Eight weeks later the captives and their captors straggled into Montreal. Here the Governor took pity on the Reverend Mr. Williams and, after two and a half years, he was exchanged with fifty-seven other prisoners, two of them his own children.

But when they went home, sorrow went with them. His youngest daughter, Eunice, who had been adopted by the Indians, was kept behind. Her adopted family refused to ransom her.

Eunice grew up heart and soul an Indian, and, when she married, the husband of her choice was a Caughnawaga chief. She returned to Deerfield to see her family, wearing the beautiful dress of her tribe. Deerfield fasted, prayed and rejoiced, grateful for her deliverance. She did not feel she was delivered, however. Her choice was to turn her back on the whites and return to her adopted people and her Indian children.

Hardly a family in Stockbridge had escaped the personal disaster of Deerfield. The schoolmaster, Mr. Kellogg, about whom the Mohawks complained so bitterly, had been a captive child taken from Deerfield. He and his sister had been reared by their Huron captors.

Jonathan Edwards, acutely sensitive to the border unrest, had been writing prodigiously, urging the English to hold, at every legitimate cost, the friendship of the Six Nations, the nations of which the Iroquois and the Mohawks were a vital part. For, he argued, if they deserted to the French as had the Hurons—at one time a part of the Six Nations—he was afraid that the Stockbridge Indians, even the gentle Housatonnucks, would follow also. The tides of war could thus turn in a moment and the Colonies would be lost by Great Britain to the French.

His was one of the voices of diplomacy that was

heard. Throughout all these battled years the Six Nations continued faithful to the British. Much of this was due to the wise young Irishman, William Johnson, who was made Superintendent of Indian Affairs in the Colonies.

He appreciated the Indian character and treated them, as did Mr. Edwards, with respect. He understood them. He was even adopted into the Mohawk tribe and made a sachem. His good friendship with the great Mohawk chief Hendricks was cemented by his marriage to the chief's sister.

Sir William Johnson's friendship with the astute Hendricks was not without several attempts at a friendly besting of the other. On one occasion, the Mohawk Chief Hendricks was in Sir William's home when he received a package from England. The packet contained some richly embroidered clothes. The Indian took a great fancy to them and, not long after, he told his host that he had had an amazing dream. He had dreamed that Sir William, as a token of his affection, had given him one of these suits.

Noblesse oblige, the gift was made, and Chief Hendricks walked about resplendent in the embroided scarlet uniform that Sir William had ordered for himself.

But there came another day. This time Sir William met his friend and wanted to share with him a wonderful dream he had dreamed. Chief Hendricks had given him, as a gesture of his abiding love, a tract of Mohawk land, five hundred acres more or less. His dream, too, came true. But Chief Hendricks wryly commented, "I will never dream with you again."

Although the Six Nations, due mainly to this close friendship of Sir William Johnson of England and Chief Hendricks of the Mohawks, posed no threat to the village of Stockbridge, there were always other Indians than "Our Indians" prowling about. French-instigated marauders were breaking through the frontier.

What concerned Mr. Edwards especially was the news he gave his family of the new scandal, an advanced price of the scalp bounty. Both sides had made the horrible practice of paying for the scalp of the enemy. In 1703, Massachussetts paid twelve pounds per scalp. In 1722 the bounty was raised to one hundred pounds per scalp. Now it was being rumored this ghastly, lucrative business was to be fostered by another hike in sales. Since an Indian scalp is an Indian scalp, no American Indian, friend or foe, was safe from the debauched frontiersman who wanted gold.

Even as they were discussing at the table this savage attempt to combat savagery with savagery, and the new dangers involved, Jacob Konkapot, a Housatonnuck Indian, entered the dining room. He was the bearer of gruesome news. The Indian Christians who had been buried in the cemetery were no longer interred there. During the night grave robbers had dug them up. They had stooped to scalping the dead.

Mr. Edwards left the family immediately, and, saddling his horse, rode out with Jacob to the cemetery. "They call the red man 'savages,' " he thought bitterly. "God have mercy on us. What of the white man, with generations of Christian teaching, behaving in this depraved way!"

At the desecrated graves he stood with his head bared. It was no wonder there were rumblings of trouble on the border. Solemnly he rode back to his home. At the gate he turned his face to this American Indian member of his own congregation, whose own mother's body had been among those desecrated. As a Christian Englishman he was so ashamed he could not speak. His face was a mute apology for his own race. He spoke no word, but the Indian understood. This impassive man the red man could read, and Jacob Konkapot knew his grievance would be redressed if it were humanly possible to do so.

As Mr. Edwards reentered the shelter of his own dining room he spoke with cold anger, "I only pray that God in His mercy will prevent Stockbridge from becoming another Deerfield. We deserve the full vials of His wrath."

11

By 1753, disgruntled Mohawks were leaving Stockbridge by the hundreds. Jonathan Edwards wrote to the Commissioners in Boston, "The last Tuesday, about two-thirds of the Mohawks, young and old, went away from Stockbridge, and are never likely to return again." It was apparent to all that if an evangelical work were to be continued among them it would no longer be possible to minister to their souls at the outpost of Stockbridge. The frontier would have to be pushed back by the white man. The man of God would have to leave the fort and pursue his flock into the wilderness.

This opportunity for pioneering fired the spiritual imagination of Gideon Hawley. A mission station was set up by the long houses of the Mohawks in the Onohquauga region where they had located. This new mission was built two hundred miles north of Stockbridge, and was adjacent to the territorial line which divided the land holdings of France and those of England. It skirted dangerously near the territory of the Huron, the tribe which was friendly with the French.

Gideon Hawley was a fiery evangelist, totally unafraid. Unlike his more cautious friend,

Jonathan Edwards, he came dangerously close to presuming on the Almighty to get him out of waters into which he waded with great temerity—often out of his depths. But this very adventuresomeness of his made him a great pioneer missionary.

Although he and missionary Edwards differed on the boundaries of where trust in God ended and presumption on the Almighty began, they were in accord in their zeal to reach the Mohawks for Christ. Jonathan Edwards preferred the slower, more lasting method, he felt, of teaching the Indians to read so that they could search the Scriptures for themselves. The trouble with a personality like Gideon Hawley was that he was too impatient to be about what Edwards considered to be part of the Lord's work. Language technicalities were bothersome obstacles to him. As long as he could muddle along and be understood he was content. It mattered little to him if he witnessed in the Mohawk equivalent of the King's English. He would lose, as a result, what seemed a unique opportunity to become professional in the language of the Mohawks.

This troubled Jonathan Edwards. Mrs. Ashley, the interpreter of the Stockbridge fort, could go on forays with him accompanied by her husband, but she would not be able to tarry long enough to be the grammatical tool he felt was so sorely needed. With his long-range vision he was irritated, yet sympathetic, with Gideon Hawley, who could only see the present harvest white-ready for the reaper.

As he stood at his study window, burdened by these cares, the chatter of voices speaking in the Housatonnuck language caused him to notice two boys, one his own son, Jonathan, the other Fleetfoot, his Indian friend. Fleetfoot was sitting bareback on his pony, holding another mount by a piece of rope. The conversation was unintelligible to him, for he had never mastered the language himself. It must have been an invitation to ride, for, as he watched, Jonathan flung himself on the back of the pony and the two raced down the village street. Jonathan disliked riding with an English saddle. He preferred to ride bareback like an Indian.

There was his answer, Jonathan. His son was more Indian than English. What an opportunity for his son! He was already adept in the language of the Housatonnucks of Stockbridge. Now he could live with the speech of the Mohawk people. Jonathan was, like most missionary children, born across the bridge which their adult parents were unable to cross. These children of missionaries had one great advantage, the gift of birth. They were born natives. The people accepted these young ones as their own. He could send Jonathan for a prolonged visit to Onohquauga. But what would his wife think? He would talk to Mrs. Edwards.

He found his wife in the kitchen helping their slave, Venus, make apple butter. Little Betty was sitting at the table, her face eloquent witness to the fact that she was the self-appointed taster of the product. Pierrepont, who always seemed to be wrapped about his mother's legs, came loose to leave one fortress in order to cling to another. Mr. Edwards sat down and took his young son on his lap.

"Mrs. Edwards," he did not stop for a breath but rushed to the end of his sentence, "I have been considering sending Jonathan to Onohquauga to live with Mr. Hawley in order that he may master the language of the Mohawks."

The clatter of her spoon made it evident that Venus, at least, had heard him, and the rustle of her skirt as she flounced about indicated her own disapproval. "It is very near the French. But no doubt you have considered all these possibilities," said his wife at last.

"I am sure Mr. Hawley, at least with the lad in his care, will exercise all caution."

"I am certain he will." His wife smiled. "He will not dare to presume for the safety of the son of Jonathan Edwards on the Almighty, no matter what risks he seems to take with his own."

"And things at present appear calm," continued her husband.

Venus pointed to the big kettle with her wooden ladle. "So does this, but watch!" Even as she pointed the mixture seethed and bubbled and overflowed.

"You are more opposed to the plan than your

mistress?" Mr. Edwards asked the slave.

"That is because I have a mind of my own. She," pointing to Sarah Edwards, "she is so sure when you speak she hears the voice of God."

"And you are not so sure," he teased.

Mr. Edwards had always treated the old slave, Venus, like a black mother. It was, he knew, she who had fought and bucked him all the way when he had accepted this "heathenish outpost." And now he was considering sending one of his own children, one of her lambs, even further out to the red man. She sniffed her scorn.

"Look at us here in Stockbridge," she chided him. Venus, who remembered the culture surrounding them in the home at Northampton, pointed out, "Your children are out picking berries like the savages. They come in with their clothes tattered. Oh yes, they know the difference between a poisonous berry and a good one. They don't step on rattlesnakes. They can ride without saddle. But is this any kind of learning for an Edwards?"

Sarah put her arms about the slave. The upset woman pulled her apron over her face to hide her tears.

"You should have stayed in Northampton, Venus," her mistress chided her.

"And let your babes loose in this wilderness?" the poor negress sobbed.

"You must remember, Venus, God led us out of Northampton." Sarah put her arm about the heaving shoulders.

"*Put* us out, would be a more accurate statement," interjected her husband wryly.

"But you had all sorts of other opportunities," wailed Venus. "You could have gone to Virginia, a civilized land. God did not lead you here," she said firmly. "And He is not leading Jonathan, my baby, to Onohquauga."

But in spite of Venus, as she had so direly predicted, her mistress sided with her master, and early in March, 1754, young Jonathan Edwards, a boy of nine, went to Onohquauga. The plan was for him to serve a two-year apprenticeship to Missionary Hawley in order to master the language of the Mohawks.

As young Jonathan packed his few belongings, the older children stood about him, in turn envying him, and in turn grateful that they had been spared this great adventure.

The young lad showed nothing but anticipation. As he rode his Indian pony out of the stockade beside Missionary Hawley, little Pierrepont, sensing like a barometer the underlying sadness of the moment, broke loose from his mother's skirts to run after his brother crying loudly. Lucy rushed after him and grabbed him, hugging him close until the thick forests closed behind the travelers.

Sarah Edwards thought of the careless people who said so casually that a child in a large family is not missed. As she often did in moments of sadness, she thought of the unfilled void the death of her daughter, Jerusha, had made. It was true that big families kept one too occupied for self-pity, but there were always those silent moments when the aching heart made its loss felt. Jonathan would be missed.

12

High palisades of logs enclosed most of the villages of the Mohawks. Young Jonathan, with his horizons broadened by this personal contact with a new tribe, was especially interested in comparisons, in how the Mohawks differed from his friends the Housatonnucks who lived in Stockbridge.

Many customs were the same. Both tribes were food hunters and had a custom of thorough bathing before the hunt in order to erase as much of the human odor as possible. They both knew that a deodorized Indian was a better hunter, for the smell of man could easily betray him to the game he sought. The Mohawk babies also were never separated from the mother parent. They slept upright, strapped in their cradle boards hung from the rafters. Jonathan had never seen a stooped-shouldered Indian. The comfortable and natural position for them at rest even from infancy was a straight back.

These Mohawks were a part of the league of Five Nations. Their symbol was five arrows tied together with sinew. This Iroquois pact was a strong one and lasted three hundred years. Jonathan grew to love this proud people. With his gift for easy adaptation, he soon felt at one with them. The Indians admired the way he walked, for he did not walk with his feet pointed outwards, as did the white man, but even as they, toeing inwards. The Indians felt that the poor white man walked as he did because his feet were crooked.

Jonathan became fat on the delicious wild turkey and succotash which was their delicacy of diet. He loved the strange wild pets his Indian friends had, and was overjoyed when Mr. Hawley let him keep the pet raccoon the boys gave him. Mr. Hawley was pleased with his young protege. Like the boy's father, he could never quite succeed in self-identification with the people whom he served. The Mohawks were his friends, but they were Jonathan's family. The boys were his brothers, their squaws his mother; and their chieftains supervised him as they did their own sons. He became so much an Indian that he confided to his guardian that he even dreamed in their language.

Much of the folk knowledge he was able to impart to Missionary Hawley. He pointed out to him the reasons for the unusual designs in the pottery and blankets of these people. The Indians, he explained, had a deep reverence for all bird life, for they too longed to secure their ability to soar into the heavens. They admired the horned snake, for, unlike man, he could shed his skin. Thus most of their primitive designs used the motif of bird or snake, and many of their dances, such as the snake dance, were an outgrowth from this veneration.

Mr. Hawley learned many of the Iroquois legends from his young friend. Among the Iroquois masks used for their festivals, Hawley knew one to be called Old Broken Nose. Jonathan told him the folklore of this mask, explaining how the American Indian, in a dim way, had a story to explain the sin of the pride of man. Old Broken Nose, the story went, got his twisted nose because he felt he was more powerful than any on earth, yea, even than any of the gods. On a high mountain, in order to prove his prowess, he sought out and found God. But in the battle he lost and God broke his nose, and he became now a humbled man. His mask was the popular one the Iroquois used to cure the sick. This was logical, for they felt keenly that all sickness is humbling, and thus a man who had been humbled by God would be a good one to intercede for them.

The man, Missionary Hawley, and the boy, Jonathan, had a rare communion with each other and their people and their God. It was an experience the grown Jonathan never forgot. As a man he wrote in his preface to his observations on the language of the Mouhhekaneow Indians, which was published in 1788, "When I was but six years of age, my father removed with his family to Stockbridge, which at that time was inhabited by Indians almost solely; as there were in the town but twelve families of whites or Anglo-Americans, and perhaps

one hundred and fifty families of Indians. The
Indians being the nearest neighbors, I constantly associated with them; their boys were my daily
schoolmates and play-fellows. Out of my father's
house, I seldom heard any language spoken beside
the Indian. By these means I acquired the knowledge of that language, and a great facility in speaking it. It became more familiar to me than my
mother tongue. I knew the names of some things
in Indian that I did not know in English. Even all
my thoughts ran in the Indian."

It was only at night that the little boy became
lonely, and it was only in the ears of his pet raccoon
who snuggled beside him in the Indian blanket that
he whispered that he was homesick, that he missed
his family.

Mr. Hawley also knew sleepless nights. The situation near Onohquauga was worsening. Hurons
were on the warpath. The burden for the safety of
his young charge caused him to consider returning
the young lad to his family. But it was the dead of
winter, and no time to travel the two hundred
miles to Stockbridge. His Mohawk friends, however, bluntly told him that if he did not risk the
journey until spring it would be too late. Impetu-
ously, one morning, they decided they would leave
at once; and with several of the Mohawk braves
they began the long trek back. The small party slept
in the open air on the cold snow at night. When
Jonathan, for all his stamina and willingness,

became unable to continue the journey, the braves slung him over their backs and carried this little white brother of theirs for miles, to bring him to his father's home in safety.

13

It was in August, 1755, that the savages invaded Stockbridge on the Sabbath Day. It was a quick foray. Between meetings they ambushed a family, killing and scalping three of them. An hour later they killed another man, a stranger coming into town, a wayfarer. Having created their havoc, the raiding party departed, swallowed up by the forest, and total quiet enveloped the frontier town. There was no doubt in Stockbridge minds that the perpetrators were a white-instigated raiding party which had strayed from their main path and done some token killing. It appeared to be the work of the Hurons from Canada, the staunch allies of the French.

Stockbridge, with its twelve settler families, was totally defenseless. It lay too close to the traveled warpath between two hostile nations. Raids such as these would become the order of the day. Total destruction was evidently not the aim of the enemy, for the village was not sufficiently important to warrant an all-out attack. Certainly if Stockbridge had been the object of a war party of Indians, by this time they would have been totally annihilated. But even such stray raids as this August ambush would in time swallow up its small population.

Colonel Israel Williams received a pathetic letter from Mr. Edwards advising him of conditions. The Colonel knew only too well that these settlers, whose main object was to convert the American Indians by piety, would be unable with the Bible to combat the vicious tomahawk of the Huron. He read with sympathy the short note from the pastor, "Stockbridge is a place much exposed; and what will become of us, in the struggles that are coming soon, God only knows."

Soldiers, the few that could be spared, were sent to the outpost to help protect the town and aid them in marshaling what defenses they could resurrect. The Edwards family home was hastily converted into a fort with tall walls built about it. It became a refuge for any terrified setter from outlying territory, and for any town residents with less security in their own homes.

During the building of the fort, kind laborers who donated their services were fed by the family. In his journals Mr. Edwards recorded methodically that Mrs. Edwards had prepared one hundred and eighty meals for the builders, and that in addition eight hundred meals were served to the fleeing refugees who passed through Stockbridge on their way to safer territory.

In addition to the temporary strain this placed on the family, rations still had to be continually stretched. For like all the families in Stockbridge the Edwards household had soldiers billeted with them. The quota of their family was four. Feeding these members of the militia, together with providing for his own large family, necessitated much foraging to secure enough food. In weakened health from frequent bouts with fever, the sick head of the home found this search for the necessities of life a great burden. It seemed at times that if one were not to be scalped by one's foes, one would be starved to death by one's allies.

These soldiers, professional Indian-fighters by trade, were typical of the colonial regiments. They were rough, crude men, but kind-hearted. They fit surprisingly well into the home life of the family. The younger children were excited by this direct contact with a world from which they had hitherto been protected, and the gruff soldiers made much of the children, especially of delicate Betty and fat chubby Pierrepont. They were lonely for their own families from whom their service for their country separated them often for years at a time.

Life with the militia did not upset the Edwards family in their daily routine of family prayers. The others were always included in their worship services. And family devotions found the soldiers kneeling on the floor on untried knees. They saved their profanity for the out-of-doors. One of the hard-core soldiers, Stebbins, when he could have moved on, requested he be rebilleted with the family of Jonathan Edwards.

With the active resumption of the war with

France, England had announced another raise in
the scalp bounty for any Huron scalp. Since all
Indian scalps looked alike, Missionary Edwards had
to spend much time preserving the lives of his own
Indians. Enraged settlers fleeing through Stockbridge, who had been made homeless by Indian
raids, salved their consciences by telling themselves
they were acting justly when they killed and scalped
profitably any man of the red race. To them, "There
is no such thing as a good Indian" was a truism.
Even some Sabbath visitors, who stood about at the
worship service for the Indians, worried the
preacher; for it seemed to him they looked at his
defenseless flock with avarice.

Anxiety for his absent son, Jonathan, began to
mount. Venus moaned around predicting the
worst. She had warned them. The fact that she had
been proved right by circumstances did not ease the
heavy pall which hung over the family. Mr.
Edwards was especially grateful now that his boy
had been Indian-trained and knew Indian ways.

To make matters worse, Mr. Hawley, meaning
to do what was best, sent by runner word that he
felt it imperative that the lad be returned home
immediately, for Onohquauga was no longer a safe
place for him. The family knew now only that
somewhere between the Canadian border and
Stockbridge a very young boy was coming home
through woods full of hostile Indians. It was
January, and one of the coldest winters Massachus-

setts had ever known.

Jonathan felt the warmth of the brave's shoulder as he hung like a slain deer over it. His face, half frozen from the cold biting wind, watched the soft prints of the moccasin wiped clean by the blizzard. It was a good night in many ways for them to make the trip. The extreme snow would keep the Huron close to his own campfire. Only a fool would go afoot on a night like this. In addition, the wind, nature's eraser, made it impossible for the enemy to track them.

The boy felt ashamed that he had not been able to walk any further, but after fifty miles of the winter's trail his feet had ceased to move. He felt now like a statue made from ice. It was as if any sudden movement snapped him in two. He was grateful when the brave gently set him down. It was too dangerous to build a fire, but the Mohawks had found a small natural shelter, a hollow in the woods where they all climbed close together, their proximity producing a certain amount of heat. They dared not sleep long. It was too dangerous to fall into a sound sleep when the snows were so cold. It could be a sleep from which there would be no awakening.

The Mohawk guide awakened him, it seemed, almost as soon as he had shut his eyes. He feared that with the coming of the sun their danger from the warring Hurons would be too great. Once again Jonathan tried to walk. Before long he faltered, and once again he was gently slung over the shoulders of his guide. The way at best was long, but because of dangers to be avoided the little company walked and then backtracked and detoured to save themselves from any silent ambush. While a white man would have plowed doggedly onward, the red man patiently darted from tree to tree and bush to bush.

It was only when Stockbridge village was sighted that Jonathan's Indian friend set him down. With the sensitivity of the Mohawk, he knew the lad would want to walk into his father's home on his own two feet.

The family was on their knees at evening prayers when the hound dog whined. "Praise the Lord!" ejaculated Venus stumbling up from her knees. The family stood quietly by while Father unbolted the door. The dog, Jonathan's Indian dog, slipped silently out the door and down the path. He knew his master was home.

14

The horizons of pioneer life were restricted by the bare necessities for survival. Much time was expended on the growing of food. Much was utilized in the search for fuel. The New England winters were severe and long. In Stockbridge Mr. Edwards tried to buy a plot of land with trees so that he could have the much-needed fuel with which to stoke his fires and keep the family warm. Homes had large fireplaces, so large that it was possible to burn large hickory logs within it. These logs were so heavy that they had to be drawn inside the kitchen by a horse, and it took two stout men to lift them onto the andirons. Usually the settee was placed on one side of the fireplace and a comfortable armchair on the other.

As you entered the homes on the frontier, you noticed a strange, savory smell made of a mixture of the flitches of dried beef and bacon, strings of dried apples and peppers, and bunches of sage and summer savory, and fennel and caraway which hung from the rafters or were nailed to the walls.

Rural social functions grew out from these essential duties of the early homes in the Colonies. The people had a togetherness about their work.

Man could not work or live alone. They met to raise a barn, or had a special woodcarting day when farmers brought wood into the yard for community cutting. There were husking bees, quilting parties, apple paring socials and singing schools. All social evenings closed with prayer, and festivities were seldom prolonged much after nine o'clock.

Home was a factory. Wool and flax produced on the farm were spun and woven on the family loom. All fuel and food were products of one's own acreage. Only in the cities did one have chairs and carriages. Here each home had its own stable of horses. One either rode or walked. Women who accompanied their husbands would sometimes ride side-saddle on pollions behind them.

School and, especially, the church was the center of all life. All families with children contributed wood, according to the number of the children, for the heating of the schoolhouse. But churches were not heated except for little foot-stoves which women were permitted to bring.

People in church were seated according to their age and quality. Deacons and older members sat closest to the pulpit. Boys were seated in a section by themselves with several constables to watch them. Long wands with which they could tap the heads of offenders were carried by the ushers. There was no organ, only a tuning fork by which the congregation could be led to sing *a cappella*. In Northampton there were slave galleries, special pews for the negro servants. In Stockbridge there were so few blacks this was not deemed necessary. The minister of the parish was honored and revered. In the church, friend and foe all stood as a sign of respect when he entered. The minister of the frontier could be personally disliked, but none had the temerity to challenge his social position in their midst.

Sabbath was strictly observed. It began at sunset on Saturday and ended at sunset on Sunday. There was a law passed in New Haven in 1643 that "Whoever neglects to attend worship on the Sabbath, Fast and Thanksgiving Days, without sufficient cause, shall be fined five shillings for every such trespass."

Those people who were not church members were disqualified from holding civil office. Even intentions for marriage had to be announced in church three weeks before the event, or published one week before by written notice affixed to a signpost, a method of publishing legal notices older than the newspapers.

Life in New England was a closely knit community existence. In Stockbridge the same pattern was followed as in Northampton, with the only difference being that there were fewer participants.

15

The settlers in Stockbridge had been chosen because of their high moral caliber. It was hoped that
by their upright Christian testimony they could offset to some degree the damage done to the cause of
Christ by profiteering white men. They were from
well-bred backgrounds. Like their American Indian
neighbors, some of them too could claim to be of
royal lineage. There were, for the size of the village,
an amazing number of Christian aristocrats. Three
out of the twelve original families in Stockbridge
had royal relatives.

An example of the duality of rich heritage, both
spiritual and social, was the Woodbridge family.
There were two brothers, Timothy and Joseph, and
their children.

The Woodbridge children had a very interesting
background. Through their grandmother Jemima
they were directly descended from John Elliot, the
Indian Apostle. He was grandmother Jemima's
grandfather.

Their father John's mother was of the line of the
famous Dudley family of England. One ancestor
had been a governor of Massachusetts. And they
were related to the Earl of Northumberland, one of

whose sons had married the ill-fated Lady Jane Grey and who had been executed together with her and that political Earl. Another in their family tree had been that glamorous Dudley of whom Queen Elizabeth had been enamored so many years.

The historically oriented Edwards children enjoyed this touch these family friends gave them with romantic epochs of the past. They knew that they too, through their mother Sarah, had royal blood, for grandfather Pierrepont was of a younger branch of the noble Duke of Kingston of England. But their lineage had nothing quite so sparkling and spicy as the Woodbridge heritage.

In addition to the Woodbridges and the Edwardses, there was also the Willard family who added their touch of aristocracy to Stockbridge. John Willard was descended from Simon Willard, who married the granddaughter of Lord Dacry, Earl of Rivers.

Although the original families chosen to live in Stockbridge had been only four in number, by the time Jonathan Edwards took up his work among them they had expanded to twelve. His own selection to the missionary outpost brought others of like mind to settle in the new Christian center which they knew would be dominated by his thoughts. It was to be, they hoped, a New England Geneva of the mind. The crudity of wilderness life was to be borne in exchange for the spiritual treats which they could give their children, a rich

Christian environment.

One such family was that of Stephen Nash. He made it perfectly plain that he had moved to Stockbridge in 1752 in order that his family could be reared under the pastorate of the Reverend Jonathan Edwards. He did not count life in the hinterland any barrier to what he considered most vital, a Christian tutelage which he wished to bequeath to his children. The presence of this family added also to the romantic legends of the settlers. For Elizabeth Nash, the mother, was the granddaughter of Lieutenant Philip Smith, a soldier so upright in conduct that it was believed in his day that he had been persecuted to death by witches.

The Josiah Jones family was one of the original four families of the settlement. Their oldest son, Josiah Jr., was almost thirty when the Edwardses moved to the outpost. Like his father, who had been selected for his piety as an original resident, he was much admired by the Indians. He was described by the red man as, "Good man, always kind to Indian."

But unfortunately all of the settlers could not be described in the same terms. There were those who, instead of helping the Indians, used them. One of these was the much-disliked Martin Kellogg, headmaster of the Hollis Boarding School for Boys.

Martin Kellogg had been introduced to his post by his sister, the popular Rebecca Kellogg Ashley, the official interpreter in Stockbridge. Misguided by affection, she had aided her brother into a post which he used ruthlessly for his own self-interest.

Both the Kelloggs were survivors of the Deerfield massacre. Rebecca, however, bore no scars from their experience. She was small and such a charming child the Indians had adopted her as one of their own. All her life she loved these adopted people and did all she could for them. Her service was considerable, for she spoke the language of the red man as only one born to wear moccasins could do. Her husband, Benjamin Ashley, a devout Christian, helped her and shared her zeal for these original Americans.

It was another story with her brother Martin. He shared her skill in his knowledge of the Indian language; his attitude, however, was totally different. In his case he had undergone the horrors of the massacre as a boy in his late teens. Rebecca, only nine at the time, had been much made over by the squaws; but he, almost a man, had known instead the rigors of the so-called games by which the Indians developed courage, fortitude, and stamina. His strong body had won the admiration of his captors. His bull-like courage aided him. But the experience had twisted his mind.

He served now as schoolmaster to the red man, and he abused the boys under his care. Never for a moment did he forget Deerfield, his massacred parents, the death march to Canada. Now it was his turn, and he worked the boys hard to make his own fields profitable. It was his ironic revenge. He made the common mistake of the frontiersman, that of not being able to distinguish between a good Indian and a bad Indian. The Housatonnucks had never been at war with the whites, and the proud nations of the Iroquois, of which his own Mohawk boys were members, had always fought on the side of the British. It was the Hurons who had captured him. But this man who was described in an understatement as "firm of mind" stubbornly threw his weight on the side of those who exploited the savages. He was not an Indian lover, he was an Indian user. He had been molded in strong fire.

There was another family among the original settlers in Stockbridge who used the situation of the red man for personal aggrandizement. Their attitude was less understandable for they had not the same excuse for their attitudes. This was the family of Ephraim Williams, who lived with his children in a home on the hill.

His daughter, Abigail, had married the first missionary, John Sargeant of Stockbridge. His relatives, fired by genuine missionary zeal, had helped open the outpost. For it was Stephen Williams who had requested Governor Belcher to grant that this mission be opened and that John Sargeant be appointed to serve it. And it was Stephen Williams who sealed the bargain with the Indians by the customary presentation of the wampum belt—a substitute for a deed on the frontier.

But seventeen years of isolation had changed Ephraim Williams. He had become possessive of the village. It was as if Stockbridge had become his town and he were lord of the manor. All went well if nobody crossed him. And gradually there entered into his attitude the realization that there was money to be gained from his situation. He saw lucrative returns from this village of his.

At his instigation, his widowed daughter, Abigail Sergeant, was appointed headmistress for a school of Indian girls and received a year's salary for a school which did not even materialize. There was no accounting to any outside audit for any mission money. Many of the philanthropic gifts got stuck passing through his avaricious fingers. And now with this newcomer, Jonathan Edwards, a systematic man and not a dreamer who could be easily fooled, appointed head of the Indian work, the way of life of Ephraim Williams was threatened. He was a dangerous man at bay.

Mr. Edwards was welcomed to his new post by all the red men. Among the white settlers feelings were not so unanimous. There was a strong hand of friendship extended to him by most, but there existed also a fist of opposition, for there was no doubt that Ephraim Williams, the dominant voice in the life of the town, was not with him. In between there drifted, as there always does, those lukewarm, timid people, neither at peace nor at war with the new missionary.

It looked as if there was no peace to be found even within the stockade of Stockbridge. The weary minister wrote a letter of consolation to Mr. Gillespie in Scotland, who was having trouble due to his firm Christian stands, "As to my own circumstances, I still meet with trouble, and expect no other, as long as I live in this world. Let us then endeavor to help one another, though at a great distance, in traveling through this wide wilderness; that we may have the more joyful meeting in the land of rest, when we have finished our weary pilgrimage."

16

The frontier, whose population if counted in the number of households of settlers was small, showed no sparseness when it came to children. Ten was a common number of offspring to have; and the eight Edwards children, who were still at home among the twelve families of early settlers in Stockbridge, counted at least forty whose age span ranged the gamut of their own.

There were the ten Nash children. The oldest, Bathsheba, was twenty-two; she and her sisters Joanna and Elizabeth were within four years of each other. All three were good friends of Esther Edwards. Phoebe Nash was sixteen. She and her younger sister Desire and Stephen were compatible with Lucy and Timothy Edwards. Young Jonathan found his own age friends in the identical Nash twins, Experience and Mercy, who were seven. The twins, he felt, were good company in spite of their sex. To complete the congeniality of the two families, the baby of the Nash family, little Rhoda, played with little Elizabeth Edwards.

The Timothy Woodbridge children were somewhat younger, with Abigail, their oldest, being fourteen, a year younger than Lucy Edwards. Sybil, who was eight, was the age of Eunice Edwards. Sylvia, a girl again, paralleled Jonathan. Timothy, William, and Enoch Woodbridge were all younger.

Joseph Woodbridge had a thriving family also—his own and those stepchildren from his marriage to a widow. These stepchildren had reached maturity by the time the Edwards family moved to Stockbridge. But many of his own children were of a companionable age. There was Jemima who was twenty. On down the scale in ages they went with Isabella, Mable, and Jahleel. Jahleel, a big strapping lad, went out of his way from the very beginning to escort feminine Lucy Edwards about, a young lady still not long in her teens. The baby of the Woodbridge family, Stephen, was never strong, and his death in childhood saddened his many young friends. The Joseph Woodbridge family home offered an ideal playground to the young people. It was a one-story house which bordered on the mill pond. Swimmers in summer and skaters in winter made this their headquarters.

There was also in the wilderness a young set of sisters—Anne, Keziah, and Abigail Jones, all above thirteen years of age, and Elijah Jones who was eleven. There was Joseph Willard, who was eleven, and his younger sisters Anne, Lydia, and Sylvia.

Like children of mission stations today, so often separated from blood kin, the isolation molded the young people into one big family. Friendships were deep and close.

The Edwards children did not play only with those who were in sympathy with their father's position. Even the Williams children were a part of their happy life. The parents of both families were at odds but, unlike the Montagues and the Capulets, did not encourage feuding to the next generation. And the children felt no estrangements growing from the unhappy situation between the adults. Esther Edwards was especially fond of the younger daughter in the family, Elizabeth Williams, who was about her age of nineteen and who shared with her many of her own romantic secrets.

The younger children of Elizabeth's older sister Abigail Sargeant were their companions also. Electa Sargeant was eleven and about Susannah Edwards's age, while young Erastus and John played with the smaller of the Edwards children.

Mr. Edwards had had a high regard for his predecessor, Mr. Sargeant, and his children, although the grandchildren of Ephraim Williams, living in his house with their mother and new father Major Dwight, were often in his own home. This courtesy was returned by the Williams family who lived on the hill. The children felt no enmity toward each other. The older members knew and understood the differences between their parents, but being well brought up they treated their elders with respect regardless of the situation, and an easy relationship was maintained among them.

One of the favorite sports of the young people in

Stockbridge was sledding over the crusted river. Sometimes the Indians would join in their fun, speeding in their soft moccasins across the frozen wastes and pulling the sleds of their friends. Another event to which they all looked forward was the weekly sing. They enjoyed getting together and playing with their voices making varied harmonious arrangments. After the song fest they would gather in one home selected for the evening and pull taffy or bob for apples.

In the summer they rode together or went berry-picking. All the children rode in the saddles as if born in one. The boys would race their ponies and often try tricks to show off their horsemanship. Most of them could mount a running pony bareback. Many of these sports they shared with Indian friends from the village.

It was a carefree existence, simple in the extreme. The calmness would be broken occasionally by a visit from older members of the family who had gone to seek fame and fortune away from Stockbridge. The older stepbrother of the Williams children, Ephraim Williams, Jr., a distinguished soldier, caused a social flurry on his visits. They also looked forward to seeing Dr. Thomas Williams return, who was now a distinguished physician. The Williams family was related through the Stoddards to the Edwards family. It was tragic that such related peoples could be at war with the other. But at times the sword of the Spirit will cut one off from one's own flesh. The situation at Stockbridge necessitated these hostilities, but it was a blessing that, due to the wise handling of the situation, the children inherited no bitterness and that all the children in Stockbridge were friends.

But even though the children in the Edwards family looked forward to their skating and sledding parties, and especially their weekly choir rehearsal with others of their own age, they also found unusually close congenial fellowship within their own family unit.

At the time of the move to Stockbridge there were eight children at home. Esther was now the oldest daughter. Mary had been married shortly before they left Northampton to tall and strong Timothy Dwight. Sarah was no longer at home; she had married Elihu Parsons. This was no mean feat, considering the fact that when her father had been asked for her hand in marriage he had felt it his duty to warn that young man that his daughter had a most unfortunate temper.

When the nervous suitor had asked if the grace of God were not in her, her father had replied, succumbing to his wry sense of humor, that there were some people with whom the grace of God could live, but no one else.

Love had triumphed, however, and Sarah and Elihu Parsons had married. They were even hoping to join the family soon and were moving to Stockbridge. Past experiences were blotted out;

however, there was a slight carryover. Elihu had a
habit of fidgeting when he was in the presence of
his father-in-law.

Esther Edwards was in, what was to her, the un-
enviable position of being the oldest marriageable
daughter of the family, moved disastrously at this
all-important age from the social life which she
loved to a rusticity with which she was unfamiliar,
and with which she had no desire of becoming
familiar. Her letters to her good friend, Sally Prince
in Boston, sustained her during her exile.

The other Edwards children adjusted easily to
the new frontier. At the time of the move Lucy was
fifteen, Timothy thirteen, Susannah eleven, Eunice
eight, Jonathan six, and Elizabeth, the fragile one,
four. Baby Pierrepont was a toddler of one.

Jerusha was dead. If the vivacious Esther
Edwards inherited her mother's charm and polish,
she possessed also a rapier wit. It was Jerusha who
had most resembled her mother in her sweet mystical nature, a rare gift she too possessed in her early
teens.

Although the family did not speak often of her,
when the family was counted it was impossible to
forget Jerusha. Her place in the large family was
never filled. Jonathan, especially, mourned for this
gentle older sister. He still counted her as a member
of the family, and he too would have stubbornly
held to the fact: "We are eleven, ten on earth and
one in heaven."

These were the children in the New World frontier outpost of Stockbridge.

17

A small but vocal minority that made up a part of the Stockbridge mission were the slaves. Most of the colonists had negroes whom they had brought with them. The Edwards family had the old family retainer, Venus, and, since she had become aged and infirm, had added the younger and more energetic black, Rose.

There was a unique situation existing in the New England colonies between slave and master. For the most part there was none of the exploitation of flesh one found in the deep South where the blacks were the backbone of plantation life, and where a greedy master, succumbing to the temptation of wealth at any price, would beat all the work he could out of the human machine he owned. The negro servants in New England were slaves in that they were bought and sold, but once bought they became a part of the family.

The Puritans felt very strongly that God had placed each man in his own station and that each man was to serve in his allotted place. Masters, however, were to function as good masters, even as slaves were to work as good slaves. They were especially aware that in the last days there would be a

95

strict accounting. Any cruelty inflicted on another child of God would be punished. Economically they were not tempted like slave owners in the South, for the economy of New England did not depend on slave labor.

Samuel Hopkins did more than any other man in New England to free the slaves, but, although he was a devoted disciple of Jonathan Edwards, his master apparently seems not to have expressed any opinion on the subject of abolition.

Venus was a faithful member of the Stockbridge congregation. She did not attend the American Indian services but went with the colonists to the one held in English. Her reason was one only—she was terrified of the red man. Even though she was aware that the American Indians who attended the Stockbridge church were children of God, she was forever afraid that they would forget this new principle within them, that they would backslide.

Even when she went to the frontier store it was noted by the family that Venus always tied a bandanna even more firmly than usual over her woolly head. She did not want anyone tempted by her fuzzy scalp and she buckled it down.

She was quite logical in her prejudice. After all, if the Stockbridge Indians were afraid of the Mohawks, and they were both red, was not she, a black woman, entitled to a color reaction?

She did not approve of the way Jonathan spent most of his hours in the Indian village, and the way he chattered away in the heathen tongue. Everybody knew that English was the language of God, and if it were in her power she would show by her behavior that at least one member of the Edwards family was preserving aristocracy in the wilderness.

Mrs. Edwards would often take a bucket of food or warm clothing to some wigwam. These people were a part of her husband's parish. The squaws were at ease with her, but they were all in awe of Venus. Venus, dutifully, would accompany her mistress, would carry the basket, but she would not speak to anyone. The little papooses stared at her with their solemn eyes.

"What do you think the Good Lord thinks of strapping a baby to a piece of wood?" she would indignantly mutter to her mistress on the homeward journey. The question, as Venus's questions usually were, was rhetorical. Venus was sure of the Almighty's opinion in all matters.

Especially in the long house of the Mohawks, Venus would search suspiciously about for any sign of fresh locks of hair. All too often she had been appalled at the scalps hanging from the rafters. These trophies of the wars, which the braves regarded as medals of honor, were prominently displayed. Sometimes at night Venus would awake with a recurrent nightmare, the vision of her scalp hanging where it had no business hanging.

Reluctantly she had to admit that, since her

master was here primarily to evangelize the red man, services had to be held for the savages; but she did not dignify them with her presence. She preferred the sermons Jonathan Edwards preached in Stockbridge to the ones she had heard in Northampton. She could understand them. Since Mr. Edwards had to preach in two of his services allowing for the time of a interpreter, even his sermons to the colonists were kept short, the vocabulary simple.

Venus was a great believer in hellfire preaching, and liked these sermons which stirred up the nest. They were not frequent enough for Venus, for actually only about ten percent of the master's sermons were on her favorite topic. Most of his sermons dealt with practical daily duties. He always found just the exact text for the need. The Yankee peddler could not sit at ease in Zion when his method of squeezing an unlawful dollar came under the pastor's scrutiny. How he labored on that shrewdness! "The proper end of commerce is . . . that men may live one by and with another and not that one may live upon another."

But the sermons that Venus found most excruciating, and hated the most to miss, were the ones the master preached on the final judgment. This hell he portrayed, what a place—where all goodness would be gone, no restraints to evil now. Those unfortunates who had served the devil all their lives would be forced to join him and his legions in an eternity with no angels to hold them back from any viciousness they cared to indulge against them. These very devils whom they had worshipped would be turned loose to torment them forever. What dreadful irony! It would be like being jailed with criminals and no bars or jailers to help. In Mr. Edwards's sermon on Romans 2:8-9 he had said, "There is no friend, no love, no pity, no quietness, no rest, no hope, in hell."

Venus would have preferred her master to have possessed a more oratorical style. Mr. Edwards never spoke hysterically, always calmly and academically. She was sorry he did not wave his hands about more, thump the pulpit, or pace the rostrum. But he seemed to manage very well by what he said rather than how he said it. There was always the memory of Enfield. In that village, in his calm way he had preached a sermon on "Sinners in the Hands of an Angry God." The content of the message had so grabbed hold of his congregation that people held on in terror to the pews lest they slip into the great abyss of hell which they saw yawning at their feet. Venus had not been at Enfield, but she had heard the same sermon preached in Northampton a month earlier. She had been sitting in the slave gallery where she could see everything and there had been no disturbance. How she hated to have missed that "moving of the Spirit." For a man who was no pulpit thumper, he had had his moments. To her regret, she had missed his greatest.

How she longed for that great resurrection morning of which she heard! There was the picture her master painted of the wicked soul which was reunited with his body. Now that body upon which so much time had been expended during this lifetime would no longer have a beautiful exterior. The resurrected body would be a true representation of the corruption within. "Oftentimes," Mr. Edwards said, "in this world a filthy soul is hid in a fit and comely body, but it won't be so when things shall appear as they will be. The form and specter of the body shall be answerable to the hellish deformity of the soul."

This satisfied the slave's idea of justice. Now some of those Jezebels would get their comeuppance. They would look the way they were. And those who had loved and served the Lord, their bodies would look like their souls, would duplicate the spirit within.

Venus loved this dream. Gone would be her gnarled hands, her arthritic limbs. She would be straight and tall. She would be Venus, a beautiful black Venus. For all her loving her master's little white babies, Venus was black, regal, and loyal. She did not want that the good Lord "should wash out her color." She wanted a white soul in a beautiful, black, celestial body.

Jonathan would see a beatific smile transfigure the slave's face. The boy did not know what inner sights she was seeing, but as his father spoke of the resurrection morning he hoped the good Lord would not change Venus one whit. He wanted her in heaven, big and fat and pillowy. He did not want to lose one pound of her, not a wrinkle.

18

Venus stood in the doorway, her arms akimbo, watching her young mistress get ready to go out-doors.

"Where are you going, Miss Esther?"

"Bathsheba and I are practicing a new duet arrangement. I am going over to her home." Esther Edwards tied her fur-lined hood tightly over her head, put on her warm coat and mittens.

"You be careful, Miss Esther, I don't take much to the likes of Miss Bathsheba. I don't want you learning any bad habits from her."

Esther tossed her head. "Venus, you know the reason you dislike her. You can never forgive her for having a name like that."

"Well, it don't seem right for a Christian. I don't know which came first. Whether Miss Bathsheba behaves as she does because she has a name like Bathsheba or whether she would be rolling her eyes at the big Woodbridge boy anyway."

Mrs. Edwards came into the hallway. "What is this, Venus?"

"We were discussing Bathsheba Nash again, Mother."

"How could any God-fearing parents name a

child a name like that and not expect trouble?" grumbled the old woman.

"Venus, remember, Bathsheba repented. She ended a good woman," argued Esther.

"Not before she had too much fun," retorted the Puritan slave.

"You can't judge by a name, Venus. Look at your own."

"It ain't my real one. My first master named me that because he thought I was such a pretty little girl. You may not think that to look at me now." The negress stood wrinkled and fat before the dainty girl.

Esther Edwards threw her arms about her. All the Edwards children loved Venus. "You still are. You are beautiful, except just now, Venus, when you scold."

"Bathsheba, Bathsheba," the old woman mumbled.

"Look at my name, Venus. I am named for a woman who anointed her body with perfumes and all the exotic oils of the orient to win a beauty contest. You don't complain about my name Esther."

Venus humphed. It was always her answer to anything, especially when she felt worsted in an argument.

"Bathsheba Nash. Then they have a Desire. If the first weren't bad enough."

"Ah, but they improve. Then come the twins, Experience and Mercy, you must remember," Esther teased. And with this parting shot she smiled at her mother, pirouetted, and slipped out the front door.

Mrs. Edwards soothed the old woman, "Bathsheba Nash is a very fine girl with a lovely voice. I like to hear her sing duets with Esther. They will be singing at the husking bee."

"That may be, as may be. Miss Bathsheba may sing good, but she don't look down enough when a man comes around. And I don't want Miss Esther getting any skittish ideas."

Mrs. Edwards perservered. "Bathsheba has the voice of an angel."

"And the heart of a . . ."

"Never mind, Venus." The old slave had a vocabulary which was pre-Edwardian, and which she exercised in moments of rare anger.

"Come help me. We must get to the soap-making today."

The suggestion was too close to what was bothering the colored woman. "No good ever came from naming anyone after a woman that takes her bath naked on a rooftop. Mark me, now."

Mrs. Edwards let her mutter. The family loved Venus dearly. They were used to letting her have the last word.

19

The wilderness parish possessed in embryo all the problems of any church group. A chronic parish problem which was present in the Stockbridge church was the presence of the hater. There will always be men who hate irrationally, or whose original cause for hate lies buried in the dim past. Such haters were the family of Ephraim Williams. Although distantly related to the Edwards family, they disliked the new minister. Their hate could perhaps be laid at the door of the young Jonathan Edwards, who as a young student at Weathersfield had estranged himself from his tutor, Elisha Williams, a nephew of Ephraim. Or it may have been due to the fact that they had picked their own candidate for the Stockbridge mission and Jonathan Edwards was *not* their man. Although their own selection for the post, Mr. Ezra Stiles, a tutor from Yale, had removed himself from candidacy, the scales were weighed against any incumbent who had not been directly chosen by them.

Another typical source for enmity lay in the situation that their daughter had been married to John Sargeant, the first minister at Stockbridge. Although her husband was now dead, the family lacked the grace to truly wish success to a man who replaced one of their own. The Christian virtue of "He must increase, and I must decrease" was totally lacking in their way of life.

Their son-in-law had been proficient in the language of the Housatonnucks. Jonathan Edwards, they pointed out at all opportunities, was not a master of the same. They blinded themselves to truth, that their own son-in-law had gone on record that he felt that the diligent hours he had spent on language techniques could better be applied by his successor to more direct deeds. They never failed when an occasion offered itself to compare with derogation the present minister to the previous pastor.

Then, too, the soil for hate was a fertile one. For the mission had been run in a slipshod fashion with little or no accounting being given of the expenditure of mission funds. Since the death of the devout-but-easygoing Mr. Sargeant and the appointment of the new man, a systematician in all fields, that way of life ended. One of Mr. Edwards's first requests was that a man be appointed to investigate the situation, and that a resident trustee be appointed to coordinate the activities of the mission, who would be authorized and approved by the Boston Commissioners.

To the great joy of Mr. Edwards the man selected resident trustee was the well-qualified Major Joseph Dwight, a personal friend. Ironically this friendship between the two men became submerged in a shower of orange blossoms. No sooner had the good man arrived to fill the new important post than he had met and fallen in love with the widow of John Sargeant, the former Abigail Williams. He carried out a successful courtship of the young lady and married into the Williams household.

If Major Dwight had been able to continue, in spite of his marriage, with a conscientious supervision of the Stockbridge outpost, the situation could have been much bettered. Instead it greatly worsened, for he capitulated to the tempting situation. His wife, Madam Dwight, became headmistress with salary of a new school for Indian girls which never materialized. He became steward of both schools, and the government bounty distribution center was his own shop.

Jonathan Edwards had hoped with the arrival of a resident commissioner that the scandalous situation of Captain Kellogg, headmaster of the Hollis School for boys, would be corrected. But the headmaster, also, was related to the Williams family, and now, by marriage, with the Commissioner. Mr. Edwards pleaded with Major Dwight for the appointment of a scholar in the Mohawk language to replace the inefficient headmaster. He indicated how the boys read English like parrots with no comprehension. Language had become for them a useless ornament. But now he had the newly appointed resident trustee, in whom he had had such high hopes, against him.

Now both men began a battle of letters back and forth from Stockbridge to the Commissioners in Boston. Both sides had influential friends. Meanwhile Jonathan Edwards continued with his work, distressed to see the money of the philanthropic Mr. Hollis, who was subsidizing the schools, misused so inexcusably.

The Trustee in addition to the income already accruing to his own family from the Hollis foundation decided to add, to the staff of Captain Kellogg, his son who was to become a teacher at the boys' school.

In August, 1753, Mr. Edwards wrote in desperation that "Between the Dwights and the Williams it seemed they wanted to establish a Dominion of the Family of Williams over Stockbridge affairs."

Charges and countercharges sped down the wilderness road. Ephraim Williams charged incompetence against Jonathan Edwards, especially pointing out his weakness in the Mohawk language, despising the fact that, unlike his predecessor, the new minister had to preach through an interpreter.

This thrust was deadly. Strangely enough, the man who was a master of the Hebrew language found difficulty with this primitive one. He found the lack of a grammar to study insurmountable. And although he could talk village talk in the vernacular of the American Indian, he was too proud to stumble along in it from the pulpit. In academic fashion he made no attempt to defend himself from this charge.

Ephraim Williams was not too concerned about the outcome of his private war in Stockbridge. His family had helped remove the minister from his large Northampton church; this ouster from Stockbridge should be mere child's play.

Then, in the spring of 1753, Stockbridge residents were awakened by screams and shouts. Always alert to an Indian attack the settlers rushed to barricade their windows, only to see the Hollis Boarding School ablaze. It burned to the ground. Fortunately no lives were lost. The puzzle remained, how had the fire started? There were no signs of invaders. There had been no follow-through of tomahawk and scalping expected from an outside raid. There was this remarkable lack of lives lost. It looked extremely like an inside job. The fact greatly alarmed the Commissioners in Boston. Could the disgruntled Mohawk boys have set the torch themselves to their own school as a vivid protest? When it became evident in Boston that not everyone in Stockbridge was content to wage a war with pen alone, they acted.

In the spring of 1754, Jonathan Edwards wrote with relief to a friend in Northampton, "Dwight is about to remove; and I hear that Elijah Williams is in a disposition to sell, our difficulties with the Indians I think are over."

20

In addition to the time-consuming and petty problems of the typical parish then as now, there always loomed in the life of the faithful pastor great theological issues. It was no other than could be expected that the one who many granted was the most influential theological voice of his day should meet strong and headstrong opposition on some of his views.

One big theological controversy that haunted the Edwards family through their ministry was the matter of the Half-way Covenant. This Half-way Covenant was exactly what its name connoted, an admittance into the covenant of grace, but only halfway. Children of believing communicant parents were, of course, considered children of the covenant and were baptized. However, according to the upholders of the Half-way Covenant, the children also of baptized but non-communicant members who did not profess a conversion experience, but did profess faith in the Christian creed, and were morally in good repute, could also be admitted into the church by baptism. However, for these parents, although baptism of their babies was sanctioned, the sacrament of communion was withheld. This was the Half-way Covenant.

Jonathan Edwards's predecessor in the pastorate of Northampton, his own grandfather, the Rev. Solomon Stoddard, went even further than the believers in the Half-way Covenant. He believed in what might be termed the Whole-way Covenant. For he felt that communion itself should not be withheld from those who wished to partake, even if they did not claim to have a conversion experience. He justified this practice in that he felt there was a blessing to be received in the partaking of the Lord's Supper whether the one receiving communion claimed this conversion experience or not. His methodology in an expanded version was much like that of some missionaries today on the foreign field who teach prayers and hymns to pagans in hopes that the words may in time convert.

Mr. Edwards finally decided in his ministry at Northampton to oppose this practice which for many years he had tolerated while working as his grandfather's assistant pastor. He had always been disturbed by the practice, but wanted to be sure of his own position before enforcing it on others. And in Northampton he at last decided to refuse to admit into communicant membership of his church any who would not confess a belief—not merely historical, but a saving conversion experience in Christ.

It was this refusal to accept adults who did not claim to have a conversion experience into church membership which shook the ecclesiastical tree. This, his enemies shouted, was merely a weapon he had devised in order to disbar any adult who differed from him, or worse still, they charged, discrimination against any whom he disliked.

In eighteenth-century America, only members of the church in good standing had a chance to advance in the government. Rather, in the manner of "rice Christians" today, who in famine-stricken lands embrace the gospel in order to fill their stomachs, people of that day wanted church membership to fulfill their ambitions. They resented deeply this attempt on the part of a minister, silent so long, to rise and bar them from the prestige which they had taken for granted.

Mrs. Edwards, who seldom lifted her voice in church affairs, felt deeply the unfair charges leveled at her husband and felt compelled to enter in the controversy. She wrote a letter to the Council of Northampton on June 22, 1750, giving evidence which she alone, the wife of the quiet man, knew. She wrote simply stating the facts and letting them speak for themselves. She was especially anxious to dispel the idea that her husband was using this disbarment to the church as an ecclesiastical tool against any who differed from him.

Her letter stated, "I, the subscriber, do testify and declare that about four years ago, not very long after Mr. Edwards had admitted the last person that ever was admitted into this church who made no profession of Godliness, he told me that he would not dare ever to admit another person without a profession of real saving religion. . . .

"And not long after, when riding out with him, (I being ill, and riding for my health), he had considerable discourse on this subject, and spake much of the great difficulties that he expected would come upon him by reason of his opinion. I asked him what course he intended to take. He said he knew not what. I asked him if he would not publish something expressly handling the subject and vindicating his opinion; he replied not unless he was forced to it, for he did [not] at all love openly to oppose his grandfather in that manner. He said to preach against him would be looked upon as a great degree of arrogance to that purpose and much more to print against him. He chose rather for the present to content himself with giving some occasional intimations of his opinions, that people may be thinking of it; as (said he) I have already done in my book on religions affections. . . ."

This admittance of members to full communion who have a competent knowledge of the Lord, and a "blameless life," although they make no profession of a conversion experience was the crux of the matter. Jonathan Edwards was a lone voice in Northampton in 1750, crying out a view to which most Reformed churches today adhere.

His acting upon his convictions cost him the must lucrative parish in New England and almost lost him the mission outpost of Stockbridge. For many who sided with Ephraim Williams in the present troubles had relatives who had been estranged by this controversy in Northampton, and who would not let the fires of their wrath die out even when Mr. Edwards ministered in this exiled post.

Jonathan Edwards was not a loner. He was an exponent of the philosophy so tritely but so truthfully stated: "A sorrow shared is a sorrow halved."

Even his children were aware of the troubles that beset the family. There was never an attempt to shield them from depressing experiences, death or taxes. This was an evil world. There was "vinegar in life." There were "frowns from heaven." The children were aware of it. And each one, when a shadow fell across his path, had been taught first of all to anxiously examine himself to discover if this were the chastening rod of God. No circumstance was considered apart from the hand of the Almighty. If, after careful prayerful analysis, he felt his course was right, he continued serene in his position in the midst of conflict.

During the distressing days in Northampton, young Mary, just thirteen, was away visiting an aunt. In an affectionate letter to her father she wrote, "The ferment in the town runs very high, concerning my opinion about the sacrament; but I am no more able to foretell the issue, than when I last saw you. . . . But the whole family has indeed much to put us in mind, and make us sensible, of our dependence on the care and kindness of God, and of the vanity of all human dependences. . . ."

From infancy the young ones were taught the value also of keeping a door to their mouths. Private affairs were shared with the family, but no confidence was betrayed. If anyone wanted to know the parents' views in a personal crisis it was in vain to prod any of the young Edwardses for an opinion. They politely told the inquirer that he would have to ask Father about that question.

This sharing of the good and the bad knit the family into a very tight unit. In Stockbridge the children were aware of the strong opposition from Ephraim Williams and Mr. Dwight to the work of their father; but their behavior toward both gentlemen was always decorous. An explosion would occur, at times privately. Especially the volatile Esther Edwards could not resist confiding in a letter to her bosom friend, Sally Prince of Boston, that the "gentleman in question should be licked." In their behavior in Stockbridge they did nothing to displease their father.

21

There had been other theological issues. Jonathan Edwards had not been spared trouble with the teenagers of his day. There had been the much publicized ordeal with the young people in Northampton over the "bad book." This examination of several youthful members of that church had been prolonged and painful.

Three boys, ringleaders, had obtained a book on midwifery by removing it without permission from the doctor's library. They had gleefully circulated it among the other young people. This nonscientific and lewd reading of the book was what had aroused a church storm. It was assumed in the eighteenth century that this was not only a family matter, but that the church would enter the affair, and that the pastor would police the culprits.

The pastor, with judicial fairness—but unwisely perhaps—announced from the pulpit the names of all the young people he wished to examine. He listed witnesses—the innocent together with the guilty—and the ensuing confusion aroused much bad feeling. In some of his own private jottings at this time, Mr. Edwards thought out loud on paper his own reservations about the matter:

"Whether the church did anything contrary to the rules of the Word of God in determining to search the matter as they did.

"Whether thereof since they did so determine to make thorough search, the committee should not go on till they think they have made a thorough search.

"Whether I ought to have gone and talked privately with them."

Whatever misgivings Mr. Edwards had privately in the matter, the issue was carried on relentlessly to its close.

It was the attitude of the young people interrogated (even more than the deed itself) which was insulting to the minister in charge of the investigation. Respect for authority was a sacred God-appointed duty of Christian youth. The violation of this could not be tolerated in a Christian church.

The young people, in the manner of youth, were not neutral. They had vigorously taken their sides. The minister had thundered from the pulpit on the subject of the justice of God. "How many of you have not only not attended to the Worship but have at times been feasting your lusts, and wallowing yourself in abominable uncleanness! How many Sabbaths have you spent, one after another, in a most wretched manner! Some of you not only in worldly thoughts, but also [in] a very wicked and outward behaviour! When you on Sabbath Days have got along with your wicked companions, how has holy time been treated among you! What kind of conversation has there been! Yea, how have some of you, by a very indecent carriage, openly dishonoured and cast contempt on the sacred services of God's house and Holy Day! And what have you done some of you alone, what wicked practices there have been in secret, even in holy time, God and your own consciences know.

"And how have you behaved yourself in time of family prayer! And what a trade have many of you made of absenting yourselves from the worship of the family you belong to for the sake of vain company! And how have you continued in the neglect of secret prayer! Therein going against as plain a command as any in the Bible! Have you not been one that has cast off fear, and restrained prayer before God?

"What wicked carriage have some of you been guilty of towards your parents! How far have you been from paying that honour to them that God has required! Have you not even harbored ill-will and malice towards them? And when they have displeased you have [you] wished evil to them? Yea, and shown your vile spirit in your behaviour? And 'tis well if you have not mocked them behind their backs; and like the accursed Ham and Canaan derided your parents' nakedness instead of covering it and hiding your eyes from it. . . ."

Jonathan Edwards had the last word from the

pulpit and in his usual thorough way left no corners of refuge for his young people in which to take
cover. The Rev. William L. Anderson on an
Edwards bi-centennial celebration said of him, "He
follows the sinner like a hound on the trail of a fox.
He not only pursued him into every hold that he
seeks, but he makes inhospitable every retreat in
the entire field." There was no foxhole safe for the
Northampton teenagers from his inquiring eye.

But they resented his tracking of them to the
ground. Unlike our problem of the twentieth century, that of the overprivileged youth, in the eighteenth century many of the young lads were already
doing a man's job. Although they were not yet spir-
itually mature and were children in their behavior,
they were, in the pioneer life of the day, forced to
grow up too fast. Their souls had lagged, in many
cases, behind their muscles. Physically they were no
longer children; morally they were. These youthful
sinners were out to get the minister. No doubt they
played their part in his resultant dismissal from the
Northampton pulpit.

But there were the other young people who
were not recalcitrant, who were strong adherents of
the church, and small pillars therein. One such,
Billy Sheldon of Northampton, died in his youth,
and his pastor lamented his death, his loss, by a tender sermon using the text of Job 14:2, "He cometh
forth like a flower and is cut down." He used this
same sermon and thought again when his own

beloved daughter, Jerusha, who had flourished like a flower, was cut down from her family circle. On both occasions the doctrine was the same. He planned to use these "words of our Lord to exhort and beseech the young people that are here present to get ready for death."

On one occasion Mr. Edwards wrote a bereaved uncle on the death of two of his nephews that he prayed that the sadness be sanctified to his family, "Particularly to those that are young in the family; that they may be awakened by it to diligent preparation for death. . . ."

Whether he scolded or whether he pleaded his aim was the same, the salvation of the youth entrusted to his care. He jotted down on a sheet of paper notes to be used for his young people to be preached at a private meeting and recorded the words of the text in Job 20:11, "His bones are full of the sins of his youth which shall lie down with him in the dust," and for the doctrine on that occasion he suggested in his notes that he develop the thought that many persons never get rid of the sins of their youth but attend them to their grave and go with them into eternity.

The young people were his lambs. He would discharge his duty faithfully to them, doing all he could to ensure that heaven be their destination. Whether he was popular with them was irrelevant.

In the manner of forthright youth, many were for and many against the pastor; both sides, also in the manner of youth, were vocal.

They played their part in Mr. Edwards's dismissal from Northampton, fomenting parental dislike of the pastor; but in the end it was mainly Mr. Edwards' view on the Half-way Covenant that ended his relationship with the Northampton parish. But there his enemies would not let the matter rest. In the manner of a cat, not content with one blow, they continued to plague this divine, even into the backwater of Stockbridge, and even there tried to urge his dismissal.

As is so often the case, the real cause for their fervent attempts to oust him from Stockbridge remained submerged. Although the reason was theological they urged substitute reasons. It seemed best to camouflage the real issues lest believers be alienated. The charge heard most frequently was that of incompetence, the inability of Mr. Edwards to preach in the language of the Housatonnucks and the Mohawks, and the necessity for an interpreter.

The honest Mr. Edwards candidly admitted this charge was true. It was almost as if, in judo fashion, he gave with the blow, using the opponent's strength to overthrow him.

The Edwards children watched these waves of battle pass like whirlpools eddying around the family. Whether defeated or victorious they remained unsinkable. They were in the confidence of their father, and they were persuaded that his position was right. They learned early that those persecuted for righteousness' sake are the blessed. These parish problems drew them closer to the Almighty and to each other.

22

The Jonathan Edwards family, and all the settlers in Stockbridge, lived that harried existence
known only to those pioneers who lived under the
shadow of the tomahawk. There were continued
minor raids from the Hurons, although in the
main the settlement was spared any major attack.
But this living daily on the fringe of fear took its
toll in anxious hours.

Some felt this way of life was not worth the
price and left Stockbridge. The Ephraim Williams
family sold its large holdings and removed, driven
away, in their case, not by fear of the red man, but
more by their defeat at the hands of the new
missionary.

The Jonathan Edwards family stayed to see the
shifting populations remove many of their problems from them; for in time Schoolmaster Martin
Kellogg left Stockbridge also. He resigned from his
profitable school finally when the patience of its
supporter, Mr. Hollis of England, was exhausted
and when his flow of currency ceased.

There were some who were sorry to see the
Williams family leave. But in the case of the
schoolmaster, whose ambitions as a teacher simul-

taneously ended when the era of profiteering in Stockbridge drew to a close, even his friends were not loath to see him go. He had embarrassed them greatly. His own sister, Rebecca Kellogg Ashley, the beloved interpreter of the mission, who understood the complexities of her brother, and loved him in spite of his faults—even she was relieved to have him absent from the village. Martin was one of those men for whom it was easier to feel affection at a distance.

As if, in a measure, to atone to Mr. Hollis and to the Almighty for her brother's avarice she devoted her life with renewed energy to do what she could to help evangelize the Mohawks. It was not a surprise to any who loved her when she died of fever in an isolated Mohawk village. She and her husband had gone with Missionary Hawley to help with their roles of interpreter. She had given her life to wipe out a debt about which she felt especially burdened. Although her own parents had been scalped at the Deerfield massacre, she was one of the first Christians in the New World to show forth the true spirit of the Master. She understood as He that they should be forgiven for "They know not what they do." Her death was a great loss to the Stockbridge community; and as was fitting she was mourned as deeply in the long houses of the Mohawks as she was in the settlers' cabins.

The population of Stockbridge was changing. Fear of the red man removed some of the settlers.

Death cut its swath. But there continued to be a flow of settlers toward the outpost, these replacements who chose regardless of the dangers to hack a home for themselves in the wilderness. For in the center of the village stood the Church, the Oneida stone of the Christians. Where God and His Church were planted His people could be at rest.

OUR FAMILY

"Every Christian family ought to be, as it were, a little church consecrated to Christ, and wholly influenced and governed by his rules."

—Jonathan Edwards

23

The house the family built in Stockbridge was spacious, ample enough to accommodate them all but also with enough room so that the Edwards home could serve as a hostel for travelers passing through this outpost, or for the many friends who penetrated this wilderness and took this hospitable home for their journey's end.

In order to finance the cost of the new house it had been necessary to sell holdings the Edwards family owned in Winchester. At the outset Mr. Edwards had hoped to live in a mission home, and he had asked for permission from the General Court to purchase land from the Indians. He had asked for two tracts of land, one near the center of town for the purpose of a dwelling, the other a plot of woodland to supply needed fuel for the winter. He had hoped to secure this property in the summer before his family arrived so that the major job of the pioneer—that of cutting and storing wood for the cold hard winter—could be done in time.

But Mr. Ephraim Williams had opposed this sale. Mr. Edwards wryly wrote a friend that Mr. Williams had spiced his arguments with "lime juice punch and wine" so effectively that the petition for the land grant was refused him.

The new house which Jonathan Edwards built on land which he was to purchase from his own holdings was no rude crude log cabin. It was a charming colonial home. The entrance doorway was covered by a small portico, and was flanked by two windows. Upstairs there were five windows to let in the light. This main house had an annex extending backward from it with a side entrance, the one most commonly used. The whole place was enclosed by a rail fence. Small fir trees, native to the area, clustered about the house, and Mr. Edwards, as was his custom, had planted an elm. Ever since the days when he had courted and won the beautiful Sarah Pierrepont under the elm tree at her home in New Haven, it was a family tradition that at each new home where he took his wife, another elm would be planted.

The Indians had a saying that he who plants trees thinks of future generations; he who plants a garden thinks of the present. It was Mrs. Edwards who showed this interest in the here and now. Every home of the Edwards family always had a lovely garden. The children were encouraged in their walks into the woods to bring back wild flowers which would then be transplanted to grow in the fertile soil of Mother's garden. It was restful to walk the garden paths by the trailing arbutus, the sweet briar rose, and the calico bushes.

The most important room in the new home was

Mr. Edwards study. It was a small room dominated
by a desk. This desk had been made to order to suit
his study habits. It was hexagonal, with the sides
slanting upward, with book racks on the flat top.
This enabled the scholar to accommodate many
large open reference books at one time. He could
simply swivel his solid cane-bottomed chair from
one side of the sloping desk to another to follow
close reference work without wasting a minute.

Habitually Mr. Edwards rose between four and
five in the morning. He broke his study day by taking some exercise, usually a horseback ride after the
noon meal. He always took pen and notebook with
him on these rides in order to note down any
thought which the stimulation of the outdoors
brought to his mind. Often he would pin small
slips of paper to his coat even as he rode to remind
himself of related ideas which he did not want to
forget. It was said that on a fertile academic ride he
would return looking as if he had been in a snow-
storm. Immediately on his return home he would
retire to his study, sit at the big desk, and elaborate
on these pinned memos.

It was important to him to have to waste no
time searching for paper, a quill pen, or a space on
which to write. His small efficient study with its
practical desk was a great timesaver for him. The
large leaves of paper on which he wrote his finished thoughts were carefully sewn together, and
the finished manuscript had the appearance of a

small book.

Jonathan Edwards had a remarkable way of shutting out secular cares and devoting his mind to pure scholarship. The shelter of his home and the privacy of his own study made this possible. It was here he found his peace. It was from this small lighthouse that the rays of his thought blazed forth to circle the globe.

24

Jonathan Edwards was a zealous pastor who never forgot for a moment that his own family was a part of that flock, and that he had been appointed to be a shepherd to these sheep also, those within his own fold. He was ever concerned for the salvation of the souls of men, all men, not overlooking those closest to him. He never for one moment assumed that his own children were of the elect. George Perry Norris describes him as a "tender brooding parent."

When David Brainerd, on his deathbed, spent his last days in their Northampton home working for the salvation of the younger children of the Edwards' household, the host minister was deeply grateful. There was no pride there, no feeling of resentment in the father's heart at David Brainerd's fear that these children of his, who had been brought up in a covenant home with its great advantages, could be lost.

No doubt there hovered always in the shadows about him the tragedy of his own grandmother. His father, Timothy Edwards, the oldest son in the family, had lived and died a stable healthy personality. But Timothy Edwards's own mother had been the infamous Elizabeth Tuttle, whose own misconducts had scandalized her New England neighbors. Finally, in desperation, her husband had committed her as insane. Elizabeth Tuttle Edwards suffered not only the stigma of madness but the added shame of having her last child disowned by her husband.

There had been other fearful scandals in the family. There had been an aunt who had committed infanticide, killing her own son. Another uncle had paid the supreme penalty and died on the gallows for killing his sister with a hatchet. As it is so often with the strain of genius, in this family also there ran this tragedy of madness. There was the "crooked" neck, a feared physical affliction which cropped up for generations to plague the Edwards descendants. It was always felt that this affliction could be the result of the firm chastening arm of the Lord.

In a remarkable way the family of Jonathan Edwards was spared during his lifetime from any manifestation of waywardness in his offspring. However, no breakaways would have surprised a father who, when absent from his family, agonized in letter after letter over the spiritual and physical welfare of those dearest to him. Constantly he warned his own of the evils of the heart, entreating the little ones to turn to God.

When the children were away on visits to relatives, the busy father felt it a matter of such importance that he always took time to hold them, if possible, up to God through his correspondence.

Grave concern for his oldest daughter Sarah, who became ill while visiting an aunt, Mrs. Huntington in Lebanon, brought from his pen these lines:

"My Dear Child, you have very weak and infirm health, and I am afraid are always like to have; and it may be, are not to be long-lived; and while you do live, are not like to enjoy so much the comforts of this life as others do, by reason of your want of health; and therefore if you have no better portion, will be miserable indeed. But, if your soul prosper, you will be a happy, blessed person, whatever becomes of your body."

Then he added a worldly note, "Your mother would have you go on with your work, if you can, though you do but a little a day . . . . [Mother wonders] whether you are well enough to make lace; if you are, she will send you a lace and bobbins. . . . The whole family is glad, when we hear from you. Recommending you to the continual care and mercy of heaven, I remain your loving father."

This daughter Sarah, in spite of recurring bouts of ill health, lived until she was seventy-six. It may be that these very precautions her father urged upon her and upon all, this God-given duty to care for the body, sustained her for a long life.

Sickness, in the Edwards family, was always a time for self-examination. Not all sickness, they realized, was to be regarded as a chastening from the Almighty, but there always lurked in the mind the possibility that this was so. "Is this a frown of heaven?" all the family would immediately ask. When it was feared that the oldest son, Timothy, had contracted smallpox on the way to school in Newark, his father wrote to him, "But whether you are sick or well, like to die or live, I hope you are earnestly seeking your salvation. . . . Young persons are very apt to trust in parents and friends when they think of being on a death-bed. But this providence remarkably teaches you the need of a better Friend, and a better Parent, than earthly parents are; one who is everywhere present, and all-sufficient, that cannot be kept off by infectious distempers, who is able to save from death, or to make happy in death, to save from eternal misery, and to bestow eternal life. It is indeed comfortable, when one is in great pain, and languishing under sore sickness, to have the presence, and kind care, of near and dear earthly friends; but this is a very small thing, in comparison of what it is to have the presence of a heavenly Father, and a compassionate and almighty Redeemer. In God's favour is life, and his loving-kindness is better than life.

" . . . If I hear that you have escaped, either that you have not been sick [of smallpox], or are restored, though I shall rejoice, and have great cause for thankfulness, yet I shall be concerned for you. If your escape be followed with carelessness and security, and forgetting the remarkable warning you have had, and God's great mercy in your deliverance, it would in some respects be more awful than sore sickness. . . . I earnestly desire, that God would make you wise to salvation, and that he would be merciful and gracious to you in every respect, according as he knows your circumstances require. And this is the daily prayer of Your affectionate and tender father."

Jonathan Edwards, the pastor-father, worked diligently to see that his own family became a part of the greater family of God.

25

The members of the Jonathan Edwards family were loyal Tories. The American Revolution had not yet torn the settlers from their British roots, yet even in 1751 wise men could see black horizons ahead and voices were raised to warn about the reefs against which the government at home was so stubbornly sailing.

An early voice objecting to the conduct of the British officers sent to the Colonies to take command over the local fighting men was that of Jonathan Edwards.

"Let them send us arms, ammunition, money, and shipping; and let New England men manage the business in their own way, who alone understand it. To appoint British officers over them is nothing but a hindrance and discouragement to them."

Jonathan Edwards was not reluctant to make influential friends in high places. One of his friends was the distinguished Governor of the State of Massachusetts, Governor Belcher. He was a good friend of the Puritans. He had strong blood ties which drew him to the movement, for his grandmother Anne was the sister of Governor Danforth and the daughter of Nicholas Danforth, who had been a distinguished defender of the Puritans.

Governor Belcher was a very literate man. He had been well schooled, having graduated from Harvard College in 1699. He was well traveled, having visited widely in Europe. During his youthful days of touring he had met and become a good friend of the young man who was to become George the Second, and he was a great favorite with George's mother, Princess Sophia. He had charm, the ability to make and keep friends.

This friendship stood him in good stead. When, after serving as Governor of Massachusetts and New Hampshire for eleven years, he was falsely accused and dismissed from his post, he went overseas and pleaded his own case before the King, his friend. He was successful in his endeavors and was promised the next vacancy in governorships. Thus it was that he became Governor of New Jersey in 1747. During this tenure he did much for the College of New Jersey, now Princeton, and was distinguished for promoting the peace and prosperity of the colony.

Governor Belcher was a Christian politician. He was, throughout his life, intensely interested in the evangelization of the American Indian, and was a good friend of those who promoted these same interests. He served God and his country in the New World. He represented the best the Old World exported of its manpower to the New. The paths of this great Governor and this outstanding divine, Jonathan Edwards, ran together because of their common fervor for the salvation of the red man.

Neither man hesitated to warn the parent nation; but things had not come to such a pass in the days in which they lived that either of them had to face the problem of whether to cut the umbilical cord which still bound them to the mother country. They were both at heart loyal Englishmen living on a foreign soil.

26

On the dresser in the bedroom of Mr. and Mrs. Edwards was the wig stand. Even in the wilderness Jonathan Edwards wore a wig. He possessed strongly this quality, so dominant in the British, that one dressed like a gentleman regardless of the situation. It was impossible for him to adjust to the easygoing ways of frontier life. For him no coonskin cap and unshaven face, and even this adornment of the wig he maintained through life.

There was not only the wearing of the wig, but the Edwards family dressed well. In Northampton Mr. Edwards, to the indignation of the local hatter, ordered his beavers from Boston. The matter of the wig and the hat, and an occasional expensive necklace for his wife, all produced their number of critics. He did not feel it necessary to bow in these matters to anyone. He was a gentleman and an aristocrat and living on the frontier would in no whit change his mode of life.

The Rev. Solomon Stoddard, Jonathan Edwards's grandfather, had adapted more fully to the informal habits of the New Englanders, and even considered wigs affectatious adornments. When his grandson became his assistant in the

Northampton pulpit and appeared wearing a wig, and personal persuasion did no good, with great vigor Mr. Stoddard had disabused his parishioners' minds that he favored this style by preaching a sermon on "The Affectations of Wigs." His grandson, Jonathan Edwards, was made, however, of the same piece of cloth, and, although he listened with respect to the sermon, he remained unconvinced of his grandfather's position and continued to wear his wig. The children seldom saw their father with his own head of hair, for at night when it was removed it was exchanged for a night cap.

Another aristocratic habit the Edwards family shared in common with other settlers of station was the maintenance of slaves. As the economy of the day seemed to demand, they always had some retainers. These slaves were treated as Christian brothers, and often with deep affection, although their pattern in the social life was not questioned. When they left Northampton Venus came with them. It would have been unthinkable to part with her. At her death Mr. Edwards recorded her passing with grief: "God had lately frowned on my family, in taking away a faithful servant, who was a great help to us."

Venus was semi-retired by the time the family moved to Stockbridge. It was Rose, a younger and more vivacious black, who did most of the heavy labors about the new homestead. Her husband, Joab, had belonged to a Mr. Hunt of Northampton;

but it was said that Mr. Hunt was so eager to get rid of his pastor that he had gladly granted Joab his freedom in order for him to follow Rose who migrated with the Edwards family, who owned her, to the frontier.

Abolition was still a new and untried word. Jonathan Edwards's position was that each had been set by God in his appointed place, whether master or servant. It behooved one to serve in his own sphere with dignity and with honor.

Rose, the newest slave, was vivacious, full of imagination and charm. She loved to tell of her early life in Africa, a land which she painted vividly for the children. They were deliciously frightened by her tales of voodoo and black magic. It was, she told them, while she had been drawing water from the village spring that slave traders had grabbed her to take with them to America where she had been sold on the Boston market.

Young Jonathan's eyes would glaze with withheld tears as she told him this story. He who seldom cried would be totally broken up by her sad story. He was so very much a home child that he felt deeply the horror of her life; in addition he had a very strong built-in empathy with people of other races. He seemed to be peculiarly sensitive, even at an early age, to the injustice of owning another human being. When, as a grown man and a new preacher, he discovered that negroes were permitted to partake of communion only after the whites had finished in the church in which he was preaching, stoical Jonathan Edwards, Jr. broke down and wept over the practice.

Rose, with her dramatic background, had found her way to service in the Edwards family because of her skill in weaving. Mr. Edwards had written her master, "My wife desires that the person that you promise to be her maid be one that is a good hand at spinning fine linen for she shall have occasion to employ her in that business part of the time."

Slaves in New England, dominated by Puritan thought, were well treated. There seemed to be little or no abuse of the blacks. Still the idea of possessing another creature was beginning to awaken Christian reaction.

Mr. Hopkins, the young admirer of Jonathan Edwards, was an early abolitionist. On one occasion he was arguing the case against slavery with his friend, Mr. Bellamy, who possessed retainers.

Mr. Bellamy, also a friend of Mr. Edwards, had vigorously defended his position. "My slave does not want to be free. He is happy with me."

"Why not ask him?" his friend challenged.

Confident, the good man did. The slave was downcast. He was fond of his master, but, when urged by him to give his honest opinion, he confirmed Mr. Hopkins's view that no one wanted to remain enslaved—even to a good master. He received his freedom on the spot.

But this question of abolition was in its infancy.

It was young Jonathan who felt most the stirrings of a national conscience on the subject. His family loved the blacks but did not free them.

It was Agrippa, the free negro whom Joab had brought with him to Stockbridge, who voiced their opinion. Agrippa the wit, the popular negro at all the weddings in Stockbridge, would say, "It is not the cover of the book, but what the book contains is the question. Many a good book has dark covers . . . which is the worst, the white black man, or the black white man? to be black outside, or to be black inside?"

Jonathan Edwards concerned himself most with the inside of the man—be he red, white or black.

27

Jonathan came skipping down the road from the home of his sister, Sarah Parsons. He was swinging a large heavy package in his hand. His sister Susannah unlatched the gate and ran to meet him.

"Have they come? The books for father? Have they come?"

"Yes, Elihu has only now brought them back with him from Boston. Won't father be pleased?"

It was the custom of the family not to interrupt Mr. Edwards when he was at his studies. But this event warranted a departure from procedure. The children knocked and tumbled together into his study.

He smiled to see them so animated and watched while they opened the bundle for him. In it were the pamphlets he had been so anxious to receive. There was also a book by David Hume. He had written when his friend offered to send him a copy, "I am glad of an opportunity to read such corrupt books, especially when written by men of considerable genius; that I may have an idea of the notions that prevail in our nation."

The opening of the packet also met the children's expectations, for Mrs. Erskine, that lovely

Scottish mother, had tucked in an illustrated children's book for them, and one on needlework for their mother. With a whoop of joy they ran with them down the street to the Woodbridge home where mother was helping with the little sick baby.

Hands across the ocean! How much it meant to this little family living in the wilderness. Father had written Mr. Erskine, "I heartily thank you for the accounts you have from time to time sent me of new books that are published in Great Britain. I desire you would continue such a favour. I am fond of knowing how things are going on in the literary world."

Scotland was as near to them as Boston. It was the custom of their father to share at length with the family news from abroad. The Edwardses all suffered with their father's friend, Thomas Gillespie of Carnock, when he had lost his parish and been deposed from the ministry. They were fully aware that he had suffered for righteousness' sake, having refused to obey the new mandate on the subject of lay patronage. He had felt strongly that only the people themselves could call a minister. His lot, suffered because of these conscientious objections, had been even more severe than those which their own father had been called upon to endure.

The whole family learned to anticipate mail from Mr. McLaurin, Mr. Robe, Mr. McCulloch and especially Mr. Erskine. For good-hearted Mrs.

Erskine, full of interest in their work among the savages, had also a tender heart for the little ones being reared so differently from her own. The Edwards children learned to expect the treat of many a storybook tucked in among the more serious philosophical works of the day. For the teenagers, *Pamela* and other current romantic novels of the day were often included.

Civilization, the Edwards children discovered early in life, was not confined to some cultural center, some geographical location. It was, indeed, rather a state of the mind. And although they found themselves in Stockbridge, cut off from the best of schools and much that life in a large metropolis could offer, because of the wide interests of their parents and the cultural conversations with erudite friends, they were more civilized in outlook than most of their contemporaries. And they were unusually sensitive to the intellectual climate of the world. While living in Stockbridge, because of their friendships across the seas they felt at home in Scotland, France, and even Boston, the intellectual Mecca of the New World.

28

Young Jonathan rode out of Stockbridge with his father to meet Mr. Bellamy, their expected guest from Great Barrington. Mr. Hopkins, Mr. Bellamy, and Mr. Edwards were all very good friends. They read each other's works critically and enjoyed exchanging comments about them. They lent books to each other from their own library collections. It was a special pleasure to look forward to this visit from Mr. Bellamy. He possessed, as one observer had noted, a "vehement earnestness," and had been described by Deacon Smith as "possessing a great sagacity for looking into the marrow of things."

It was the family custom to greet and "Godspeed" the parting guest not at the garden gate, but to ride out at least three miles with them. Young Jonathan loved the road to Great Barrington, with forests dense with scrub pine and interspersed with tapering white birch. Especially he enjoyed the return home and the ride on the crest of the hill.

This view from "The Hill" which rose north of the town was his favorite. The path was cut along its brow and the panorama below was constantly changing. At one moment beneath one could see the winding Housatonic River fringed by willow trees dividing meadows from forest, the lovely "Ox Bow" bend. Looking north one could see another of his favorite spots, the pond one mile long and half a mile wide, very fittingly called "Mountain Mirror." To the south lay still another body of water, "Mohawk Pond," sparkling through an opening in the Stockbridge mountains.

The village itself was cupped by mountains. On the south they towered rugged and craggy. This "Fisher's Nest," as the Indians called the crags, had at its foot the pile of stones said to be the grave of a lovely Indian maiden. This young beauty had been forbidden to marry a youth who was a cousin, and hence outside the range of her legitimate choice for a husband. Desolate and despairing she had decked herself with wild flowers, and singing a wild death chant she had leaped to her death from its highest point.

This legendary story colored the attitudes of the Indians. It was customary for one, when overcome with grief, to exclaim, "I will jump off Fisher's Nest." Every Indian who passed by the alleged spot would add a stone to an ever-growing monument at the foot of the crags. For many now the reason for so doing had passed away. It was no longer a memorial tribute to an unhappy Indian maiden. Rather it had become for most Indians an expression of thankfulness to the Great Spirit for a safe journey completed. When an Indian cast his stone, he felt safe, for he was home at last.

From the crest westward one saw cupping the village Stockbridge Mountain. On the north the cup was continued by the Hill of the Wolves, as the Indians called it. Although this mountain was two miles long, it was incorporated in the town and easily accessible to the children who enjoyed exploring its many caves, especially the deep cave slashed in its side. Southeast, the geographical cup was completed by Beertown Mountain. Then, suddenly, the rim of the cup broke open, as if to let in the morning sun. This cleft region abounded in glens, natural waterfalls, and distant undulating hills. How pleasant it was to ride out three miles in any direction with a guest.

But there was also danger in these rides. The English called the Hill of the Wolves the Hill of the Rattlesnake. Here the sensitive horses walked warily in the thick woods. Instinctively they sensed that unless they carelessly stepped on a nest the snakes would glide away from their pathway. Prone to attack only in defense of young or in self-defense, the rattlers were harmless to those horses who trod gingerly through the fallen leaves. Young Jonathan would keep his eyes on the adjacent rocks upon which the cold-blooded reptiles would sun; and he kept alert for any warning rattle.

The most wonderful aspect about the company which continued to arrive even in this wilderness was the festive spirit any guest brought with him into their home. All the candles in their reflectors on the walls were lighted, and in the living room by the desk the T-shaped tall wooden candleholder would find all six long tapers lit.

Light was gala. The family usually frugally hoarded its supply of candles, going to bed whenever possible with the approach of darkness. But hospitality was God-ordained, and a duty which they all enjoyed. Even father, who usually ate alone and appeared only to say grace before and after each meal, would stay with them to eat. He always ate sparingly for his digestion was easily upset; for this reason he found eating in solitude more suited to his needs. But when company came he would be with them and sit at the head of the table, a gracious host.

29

Sarah Pierrepont Edwards, Mrs. Jonathan Edwards, was genteel. She was descended from a socially acceptable lineage. Her grandfather, John Pierrepont, Esq., came from England, and was of a younger branch of the distinguished family in the Old World. Her own father was the Reverend James Pierrepont, an eminent and pious minister in New Haven. Her mother, Mary Hooker, was the daughter of Samuel Hooker of Farmington, and the granddaughter of the Reverend Thomas Hooker of Hartford who was often called the "father of the Connecticut churches."

She had all the social graces, having "been to the manor born." In addition she possessed great beauty. Dr. Hopkins said of her, on seeing this wife of Jonathan Edwards after she had already borne seven children, "She was more than ordinarily beautiful."

She was extremely pious. This quality, so rarely to be met with in life, was hers even more uniquely in that she was distinguished by it in her early teens. It had so attracted the young ministerial student, Jonathan Edwards, that he had written of her, "They say there is a young lady in [New Haven] who is loved of that Great Being, who made and rules the world, and that there are certain seasons in which this Great Being, in some way or other invisible, comes to her and fills her mind with exceeding sweet delight; and she hardly cares for anything, except to meditate on him . . . she has a strange sweetness in her mind, and singular purity in their affection . . . you could not persuade her to do anything wrong or sinful. . . . She is of a wonderful sweetness, calmness and universal benevolence of mind . . . . She will sometimes go about from place to place, singing sweetly; and seems to be always full of joy and pleasure; and no one knows for what. She loves to be alone, walking in the fields and groves, and seems to have some one invisible always conversing with her."

Sarah Edwards had been only thirteen when this analysis was written about her. This quality for seeking out God in mystical communion remained with her through life. She did not permit this soul communion to interfere with her daily duties and tasks, but somewhere in her busy schedule there was always time for a quiet walk with God. The children early learned to respect their father's study hours, but they also recognized these times which were necessary for their mother, these moments when she needed to be alone to lose herself in God. They sensed their mother was Martha; but also she was Mary who sat at the feet of her Lord.

Others outside the family circle noticed this spiritual quality of hers. On one occasion a minister, the Reverend Mr. Moody, was offering the opening prayer at a service which was scheduled to have the Reverend Jonathan Edwards as the speaker. He had not yet arrived when the good man began his prayer. His enthusiasm for Mr. Edwards, and Edwards's apparent absence, caused the pastor to eulogize the supposedly absent party. While his eyes were shut Mr. Edwards slipped into his place. Mr. Moody, on the close of his prayer, was embarrassed to discover his words had been overheard, but hurried on to assure Mr. Edwards, "I didn't intend to flatter you to your face; but there's one thing I'll tell you: they say that your wife is going to heaven by a shorter road than yourself."

Certainly it was a less thorny way. While her husband wrestled with the great theologies of the faith, Mrs. Edwards walked like a child with her God, frequently ecstatic to be with Him.

The face she turned to those about her possessed this serenity she absorbed from these quiet times. Amazing but true, it seems to be the fact that in raising a house full of children Sarah Edwards had never been known to raise her voice. Yet she controlled her children. It was said she never let the children taste the heady wine of disrespect. It was axiomatic with the household that parents were respected. All the children rose when any adults, including the parents, spoke to them. They learned obedience with their first steps.

Sarah Edwards had this same firm, quiet manner with her own domestic help. She treated her slaves with appreciation but with dignity. She maintained a distance between them as she felt befitted the scriptural order, the difference between servant and master. She felt, however, that all men, although different in station, were equal in the sight of God; but her upbringing made it difficult to practice this Christian principle. She confessed she had trouble regarding a slave as her equal in the sight of God. She was troubled by her disobedience to God's clear teaching on this matter, and, after much wrestling with her conscience, she finally reached, she announced, that state of grace where she would not only permit but would be happy to let a negro slave precede her into heaven. Her slaves were tenderly cared for and loved, but they sat in the slave gallery in church and did not sit with the family.

One man upon whom she made a profound impression was the evangelist George Whitefield. He made one short visit in their home and found all the latent fortifications he had built against entering the marital state crumble about his ears. The bachelor evangelist could not resist this unusual combination of piety, gentleness, and graciousness. This eloquent evangelist of whom Garrick had said, "He could move men to tears, or make them tremble, by his simple intonations in pronouncing the word, Mesopotamia," was prodded into renewed activity that he too might taste the wedded bliss which he felt his friend Mr. Edwards was enjoying. In his own words he wrote, "She is a woman adorn'd with a meek and quiet spirit; [she] talked feelingly and solidly of the things of God, and seemed to be such a helpmeet for her husband, that she caused me to renew those prayers which, for months, I have put up to God, that he should be pleased to send me a daughter of Abraham to be my wife."

It was the blended quality of piety and gentleness which especially endeared Sarah to her family. Her husband's own sister, Jerusha, had possessed this same combination. She, the gayest of the big family of girls which surrounded the growing boy, was extremely devout and gentle. She was known to be acutely sensitive to the hurts of others, and especially attentive at social functions to those who were being ignored by the careless. This tender care had extended even into town to all the "beasties," the animals she met.

His sister Jerusha, as a lad, had held her brother's heart. In Sarah Pierrepont, Jonathan Edwards found repeated the same endearing graces. The only fault he could find with his wife was that her love for him exceeded, he felt, the bounds of detachment. She loved him so much she could not be fair to others. It hurt her cruelly to see any closer to the kingdom than he. She was quite certain that no one could be. He, in his forthright honesty, was equally certain he was not by any means the first in the kingdom of God.

This was her besetting sin. This desire was not for material advancement, but her great yearning was that her husband be God's chosen instrument for any great moving of the Spirit. She was not jealous *of* her husband but *for* her husband. In the early days of her marriage she had not been kind and prudent in her conversation with one Mr. Williams of Hadley, whose successful work in the kingdom momentarily rivaled her husband's. She had been crushed by her husband's few words to her on the subject. A frown from her husband upset her almost as much as a frown from God.

As the years passed, the young wife realized this attitude was not one becoming to a Christian matron. And by the time the mature Sarah moved to Stockbridge she had been able to write that she was strong enough now to withstand even the "ill will" of her husband. Any "ill treatment" from any other had never been her problem. In Stockbridge she knew with the wisdom of the years that the only godly fear was for the "frowns of God."

This Sarah who walked with God also walked in the fields. Head in the clouds, her feet never left the earth. She remained a practical wife. She taught her children all the useful pioneer duties. She devoted much time also to teaching the girls to do embroidery work, so lovely that these projects always served as sources of additional income. Their work could compete with the professional laces of the day.

Although gracious, Sarah Edwards was inclined to be diffident with strangers. She did not reveal herself quickly to others. The American Indian, with his silent temperament, was drawn to this quality they shared in common. They made no secret of the fact that they loved Sarah Edwards.

Although her intense loyalty to her husband prevented any friendships with those who were his enemies, throughout their married life the source of these quarrels lay with him. They did not stem from her.

She was a strong woman and her family depended on her. Whenever a child needed her she would go. Even when her children were grown with families of their own, a cry for help never went unheeded. From the wilderness outpost she would rush to be with them. Her husband, who shared her concern for the children, nevertheless was woefully lost in her absence. In desperation, when she was away on one of these errands of mercy, he wrote to her:

"We have been without you almost as long as we know how to be."

Sarah Edwards loved and was loved. She was a fulfilled woman.

30

Esther Edwards, the oldest daughter still at home, did not like Stockbridge. She remembered life in the city. She had drunk too deeply from its wells of gaiety and stimulation to ever be tempted to exchange its waters for the stagnant pools of this primitive stockade village. Northampton itself had been only an oasis in her life. Her real Mecca had been Boston; that thriving metropolis with its drawing-room culture had made a disciple of her when she visited her friend, Sally Prince. This move of the family away from the center of civilization chafed her, for it was in the other circles that she found her milieu.

She simply could not understand her older sister, Sarah Parsons. Her father, she knew, had felt called by God to work in this outpost. The voice of God explained his choice. But Sarah and her husband had chosen to follow them inland. Sarah, whose strong mind made up for any frailty of body, had been stimulated by the challenge of the pioneer. Of this Esther was convinced. For she was equally sure that if her older sister had not wanted to come to Stockbridge, she would not have done so. Elihu, her husband, was putty in her hands. All

the work of mother and father to train her for the
role of woman in domestic life had been totally un-
done after a year of marriage to the indulgent Elihu.
No doubt this is what her father had feared when
he had counseled the young man against marriage
to his daughter. He had realized that Elihu's kindness could and would be abused by his own strong-
willed daughter. It was Sarah Parsons who made
the decisions. Sarah had moved to Stockbridge
shortly after her parents settled there. For all her
strong-mindedness Sarah was, in many ways, the
most dependent of the Edwards children. She
wanted to be near her family and she was.

Esther had to admit she was the most grateful.
She and Sarah and Mary had always been an intimate circle within the larger radius of the family.
Mary and her husband had been left behind in
Northampton. It was pleasant to have an older sister within reach. To herself, Esther admitted, Sarah
stood as a constant object lesson to her, a typical
pioneer housewife. Esther did not want to become
like Sarah, living a life revolving around the making of apple butter. And although her charm and
spirit attracted many a buckskin suitor or migrant
missionary, Esther would not permit her heart to
become involved. Her first love was the city and its
attendant civilized pleasures. With her usual
forthrightness, no one was left long in doubt about
her state of mind.

Although Jonathan Edwards did not hesitate to

warn a suitor of the deficiencies in a daughter when he deemed it necessary, he was equally just with his girls. He did not urge the suit of any young man who wanted to court, even when he must have been tempted to do so.

Gideon Hawley, a favorite visitor to the Edwards home, did not end up a son-in-law. He had had the advantage of propinquity. After the headmaster of the Hollis School, the much-disliked Martin Kellogg, had resigned his position, he had come to Stockbridge to replace him as the village schoolmaster. It had been too late to save the ill-fated Hollis Boarding School. Factions were alive that gave him no chance for success. A friend of Mr. Kellogg's visited the school and, with no provocation, caned the son of a sachem. Incident followed incident and the school which had started with such ideals dissolved under the unfortunate conscientious Mr. Hawley. And, since he had identified himself with the Mohawks, when they migrated it had been a logical choice that he be the missionary to go with his flock.

He remained in Stockbridge only a short time, but long enough to come under the bewitchery of Esther Edwards. But it was not Esther who accompanied him to the frontier cabin, only her baby brother, Jonathan, for the erudite reason of learning the Mohawk language. His beautiful sister had no intention of spending her life in a sun bonnet.

Samuel Hopkins, another great favorite with

her father, received no help in his hopeless pursuit of his daughter. Samuel Hopkins had said of Esther that she was "formed to please." But alas, she did not choose to please him. He was, notwithstanding, always enthusiastically received by the household, but not to the extent of his dreams.

His path had crisscrossed that of the Edwards family for many years. He had been convinced that he was not a saved man, that he needed to be genuinely converted, by David Brainerd, the betrothed of Jerusha Edwards. That eminent missionary saint had convinced him that he lacked true faith. The conscientious Mr. Hopkins had become deeply distressed by his state of heart. He started out to ride to school to study theology under Professor [Gilbert] Tennent, only to have a sudden change of mind en route. With his usual abruptness he turned his horse about and rode eighty miles in the opposite direction to Northampton to seek out Jonathan Edwards. This man had spoken so logically at his commencement exercises that his mind had been totally captivated by him. He arrived unannounced on the Edwards doorstep.

Jonathan Edwards, sensing the fire and spiritual greed of this young man, had accepted him warmly into the home. He had stayed in Northampton in order to study privately under the tutelage of his chosen mentor.

Samuel Hopkins was immense in size. He had an honest face and a ponderous voice. He was strong and loud, always shouting his opinions. He was especially vehement in championing the cause of the underdog. A good deal of his voice was used in the early days to fight the battle to end slavery. His own unique idea on how to solve the difficult question of what to do with an emancipated race was to Christianize the freed slaves and return them to Africa in order for them to serve as missionaries to their own people.

The girls loved to listen to Samuel. His type of personality was alien to them. None of their brothers had the bombastic vividness of this towering giant. It may have been this very bigness that defeated his pursuit of Esther. She may have seen in Samuel a man too far removed from the personality of their own father whom she admired so greatly. Samuel had none of the refined Englishman about him. He had none of this delicate feminine quality in his being. His was a strength well suited to the rough pioneer days.

It was a tribute to both sides that his defeat in love dampened his friendship with the Edwards household no whit. He possessed no false embarrassment. This was always the way with Esther's suitors. Her vicissitudes with them did not alter the enthusiastic reception they were assured of receiving from her parents and the other children. Even Esther was so honest yet so gentle with them they were left with no bitterness towards her. It had been an honor to have been in the running with one so "formed to please." Thus the difficult bridge between a rejected suitor and a welcome guest was made easy by this hand of friendship which remained steadily outstretched to them.

It was no surprise to anyone when Esther finally made her choice. She decided to marry a man tailor-made to specifications: an older, sophisticated, charming, brilliant gentleman, no less than the cultured and erudite president of the College of New Jersey, Aaron Burr. The problem was to let the man in delicately on the secret.

She had always known him as a family friend. Whenever moments of great decision had come into Mr. Burr's life he had sought out, whenever possible, his admired friend Jonathan Edwards. He had frequently been a guest. He had held the adorable curly-haired Esther on his lap. He had seen her grow into a startling beauty. He had seen her discard suitor after suitor through the years. His modesty kept him from pressing his own suit. He was an older man, a short man compared with the tall Jonathan Edwards. He could not see in himself the quality which captured Esther Edwards. His face, like that of her own father's, had that same delicateness of feature that artists were prone to draw in sketching the face of John, the Beloved.

Esther had always maintained, "The one quality I must have in a husband is that I may admire him." Although there was much to admire in Samuel Hopkins, his hugeness of body and voice

were apt to provoke the mischievous Edwards girls
to mirth. Esther did not want to marry a man another found amusing. She wanted to look up to a
star and to marry one. This latter achievement took
considerable doing on the part of the accomplished
flirt.

31

Sarah Edwards stood beside her daughter and watched Venus brush the thick, black hair. This was the prettiest of her brood, and today she looked her loveliest. Esther had a delightful way of reflecting happiness in her face; she was totally transparent. Her mother took the brush from the slave and helped arrange the hair.

"Mother, oh, do let me wear it up the way you do! I am tired of wearing it down my back like a school girl."

"And why this sudden urge to grow up? Could it have anything to do with the visit of a certain gentleman from New Jersey?"

"Mother, when will he ever notice me? I am always so dreadfully afraid when he sees me that he will pat me on the head or tweak one of my braids."

Sarah smiled. "Mr. Burr has noticed you are grown up."

"Then doesn't he want me? Why does he not speak for me to my father?"

"There may be some other more suitable maiden in New Jersey. I am sure Mr. Burr is a bachelor not for the lack of applicants."

"Another girl—more suitable," wailed her uninhibited daughter. "How could that be? Oh, Mother, please do not speak lightly of this. Do you really think so? Do you honestly think his heart is given to another?"

Mrs. Edwards smiled at the new Esther. This daughter of hers, who had always only to reach out a hand and a suitor was in her palm, now had her own heart ensnared by the apparently unaware and unattainable bachelor, Aaron Burr, and all her self-confidence in her own coquetishness had faltered.

"I do not think he loves another," she reassured the eager girl.

"What makes you say that, Mother?"

Her mother twisted the thick hair about her fingers. "The way he looks at you, my child."

Esther blushed and threw her arms about her mother. "Tell me, tell me again. How does he look at me?"

Venus broke in, rolling her eyes, "He looks at you as if the night was black and you was the only star."

Esther threw her arms about the colored slave and whirled about with her.

"Mother, when will he speak for me?"

"Shall I ask your father to speak to him?"

"No! No! You mustn't. That would spoil everything. I don't want to be married because I am the daughter of Jonathan Edwards, and because my father proposed for me. I am sure he could refuse Mr. Edwards nothing, not even marrying me!"

Her mother laughed. "Then you must just wait, patiently. Patience, Esther."

"Did you have to wait so long for my father to propose to you?"

Sarah smiled. "No. Your father was in the mood to marry. He was a minister, a young and good-looking minister. He needed a wife."

"I know that story only too well," her daughter lamented. "He was in love with you. That must be the trouble. Mr. Burr does not need a wife. He has been a successful bachelor too long. And he is not in love with me."

Her mother stroked the beautiful glossy hair. "It will be as God wills, Esther. Meanwhile let us try pinning up your hair this evening."

"Let us, by all means, help the Almighty!" said Venus irreverently, her mouth full of hairpins.

That evening Aaron Burr rode up on the hunter Nimrod. The horse was mottled on the back and sides, a beautiful and spirited animal. The children ran out to greet him. Jonathan held the stirrups and patted the hunter's huge, heaving flanks. Mr. Burr had been in a hurry to get to Stockbridge. Even while Mr. Burr thanked the lad and put his arms about the children his eyes were searching for one who was not in the crowd. Then he saw her standing in the doorway with her mother. Her dimity dress puffed out, emphasizing her extreme slenderness. His dark eyes smiled as he came over to pay his respects. Esther became radiant.

But that evening found him closeted with her father. Esther lit the candles on the candelabra and stayed up as late as propriety would permit, hoping he would come out of the study and spend some time with her. Disheartened, at last, she blew out the tapers and went to bed.

Sarah had been asleep. She felt her husband let himself down lightly on his side of the bed. She always slept on the verge of waking, and although he tried not to disturb her she stirred.

He lay beside her telling her of his long conversation with Aaron Burr, especially this new great honor which had been offered him, the assumption of the presidency of the College of New Jersey. Only as an afterthought he added, "I am distressed. I fear he is in for a great disappointment. He has asked permission from me to ask for Esther's hand in marriage."

"Mr. Edwards. Are you sure?"

"What do you mean, am I sure?"

"Surely, oh surely, you did not try to dissuade him?"

"Dissuade him? No, why should I? Esther is not another Sarah. She would make him a good wife. I said nothing, but I am concerned. He is so sensitive and I would not have him hurt. Esther has turned away so many. I only wish he had not fallen in love with her."

"She is in love with him."

"You must be mistaken. I saw no signs of it."

His wife smiled. "We have spoken of it."

"But why did she not tell me?"

"She did not want any insinuation of the thought of marriage to have been planted by you."

"But he has been hinting about his feelings for her to me for years."

"Oh, Mr. Edwards! Mr. Edwards! And she has been telling me for years of her own unrequited love."

"And I gave him no encouragement. I was afraid she would rebuff him."

"And I gave her no encouragement. I was afraid his emotions were given to another."

"We are not, either of us, I fear, cut out for the delicate role of matchmaker."

Sarah rested her head on his shoulder. "Esther, at least, will have her wish. The idea will have sprung from no one but her suitor. The waiting has been good for her. She has had too many plums drop into her lap. This is one for whom she has had to reach. I must go and tell her the good news." She stirred in bed.

"What, and betray his confidence to me?"

"A woman does not like to enter into such an important situation unprepared. No doubt he will have his proposal speech in readiness."

He held her with his arms. "She needs no preparation. All she need say is 'yes.' Anything else of eloquence I assure you the young man will not remember."

"Did I merely say, 'yes'?"

"No. You said, 'I must speak to my father.' And when I replied that I had already spoken to him, you replied, 'I must ask my mother.' And when I told you that I had already spoken to her, and anticipating your next statement, assured you that your brother also had been approached, you replied, 'Then I am the last to be asked.'

"You are the last to be asked," I said. "The others have given their consent. Now you alone must give the final answer.' But do you remember?"

Sarah laughed. "How well I remember. My mother had been warning me for close to a year of this impetuous seminary student who would not long be put off. Also I had had my acceptance speech in readiness for some time." She quoted it to him primly like a memorized script. "I am honored to be asked. I shall be happy to be your wife, Mr. Edwards."

" 'Yes' would have done as well."

She ran a long slender finger up the deep hollows in his cheeks. "I hope they will be as happy as we have been."

He took her hand in his and kissed the open palm. "That would be unlikely, Mrs. Edwards. Ours is an uncommon union."

32

"A letter from Mary!"

Susannah rushed into the girls' bedroom to give it to them. Lucy and Esther shared the big airy front room. It had homespun woolen curtains at the windows and each girl had her own canopied bed. The only other furniture was a pair of cane-bottomed chairs and a small writing desk. Esther lay sprawled on her bed reading an old letter from Aaron Burr. At times she would share a line with her less experienced and curious sisters.

It seemed strange to think that Esther was in love. For years the younger girls had watched her toss her pretty head and play the coquette with the boys who courted her. And now this serious older man had won her, so much so that it seemed she lived from one of his letters to the next.

Esther stopped reading. "Nothing from Mr. Burr?" Her face fell.

"Don't you want to hear from Mary?"

Rebuked, Esther joined the girls as Lucy tore open the letter. They clustered about her chair. Mary had always been a favorite sister of them all. Unlike their sister Sarah, their oldest sister, who had in common with so many first-borns a tendency to boss, Mary had an easy disposition and they felt no tensions with her. It had been the hardest wrench of all, moving to Stockbridge, to move away from Mary, for in Northampton she had lived practically next door.

Mary possessed also the added allure of a handsome and charming husband. Lucy's young romantic heart turned somersaults in the presence of this glamorous brother-in-law. The more learned choice of her sister Esther failed to excite in her the romantic reactions which Major Timothy Dwight stirred. This husband of her sister Mary was well over six feet tall, muscular yet graceful. In addition to more than his share of physical attributes, he also possessed wealth, for he was a successful trader and a large landholder. He was also a power in the town, for he served as selectman, town recorder, register of probate, and a judge of the court of common pleas.

His father had the reputation of having thrown the stone the furthest of any man alive. This was the great test of strength in pioneer New England, this ability to shotput. His record of eighty rods, in all about 1320 feet, stood even against his son's assaults. Timothy, like his father, was a strong man; but what had appealed to the Edwards family and won Mary was his strong heart. It seemed impossible for him to be unkind to man or beast. If the silly attentions of Mary's younger sisters worried him, they never felt other than welcome in his home on

King Street.

Now, although geographically they were only sixty miles away, an ocean might as well have separated them. For the wilderness road between Northampton and Stockbridge was distinguishable only by the marks which had been cut upon the trees. This ocean of trees separated them as effectively as a large body of water.

Mary's pregnancy made a visit from her impossible, for there was as yet no carriage road; and even if she rode on a pillion behind Timothy her present condition made that precarious, for she had not been too well with this pregnancy. Her father had always been very cautious not to court sickness and had trained his daughters the same way.

Reading her letter aloud was too slow for the impetuous Lucy. She raced ahead with her eyes and gave her sisters the main import of the letter.

"She wants one of us to come and stay with her, if Mother cannot be spared to help."

Esther rejoiced, "Oh, I hope Father chooses me!" There was no doubt among the girls that the request would be answered and that one of them would be sent.

"You do not like it here in Stockbridge, do you, Esther?" Susannah asked wistfully.

Esther went to the windows and switched together violently the woolen curtains as if to shut out the hills she did not wish to see. "I hate the wilderness. If only Mr. Burr would hurry. I want to leave as quickly as possible."

Susannah threw her arms about her older sister and started to cry.

"No, Sukey darling. You must not misunderstand me. It doesn't mean I want to leave you. It is just that I am so restless here. You little ones are wilderness-won. You have your horses, and your skating, and your walks. I am old enough to remain faithful to the city with its concerts, its promenades. But never fear, Mr. Burr is a cautious man. Alas! He will not rush me away from you."

But it was not Esther, it was Lucy who was chosen to go in answer to Mary's request. Their mother decided not to answer the invitation herself for she was anxious also over the health of her oldest daughter, Sarah Parsons. This daughter, too, was expecting a child any moment, and she had a history of ill health. Both Father and Mother felt it wisest for her not to be away from Stockbridge at this time.

Lucy, wild with joy, clambered on the pillion in back of her brother-in-law, Elihu Parsons, who was to make the journey with her. Esther watched wistfully while the wilderness path, the path back to the city, opened up before them. But her little brothers and sisters called gleefully from the stockade, "Lucy, Lucy, don't forget to send some chocolates!"

33

Mrs. Edwards was to accompany Esther for the wedding. This epoch in her life was the strangest experience Esther had ever known. She was caught as it were between two magnets—one drawing her to her betrothed, the other to her own family. In spite of all her protestations of her dislike of Stockbridge, it was her parental home; and when the time came to leave she found herself reluctant. The delight of a permanent reunion with her betrothed was offset by the grief at leaving her family and her beloved parents and sisters and brothers. Their home would never be her home again. She would return, but it would always be as a visitor.

They took the turnpike to the Hudson, a road but recently mended. Their way went via New York where the mountains crowded to the river, and where the winding Hudson became almost as wide as a lake. As they rode, her mother watched the furrows deepen in her daughter's wide brow. She knew only so well what Esther was feeling. How deep as a girl her own attachment had been to her family in New Haven; and when her fiance, Mr. Edwards, had sent for her at sixteen, she had wanted to go to be with him in Northampton, yet was torn with longing to stay. It was her own mother who had pointed out to her the wisdom of an immediate decision.

Mrs. Pierrepont had known men. With great practical wisdom she had told her daughter that, when a man was set to marry, any unnecessary pro-longed delay was a frustration. Many a wedding, she had declared, had never taken place because of a frivolous postponement of the date for the nuptial vows.

Mr. Edwards had been the new assistant pastor at Northampton. He could support a wife and he wanted one. The delicate, sensitive man was in love with her daughter, Mrs. Pierrepont knew, but she also realized there was scarcely a mother in the large congregation with a marriageable daughter who was not entertaining hopes for the young man. A man in the ministry was an easy target for marriage-minded mothers, and even older but still hopeful spinsters would declare open season on him. A wife's presence would automatically end the harassments of those who wanted to add a man of the cloth to their own family circles. As to those other women, the troublesome ones to whom marriage would mean no barrier, a good wife could help here also. She could help ferret out these twisted ones to whom a man of the cloth presented an irresistible challenge. Above all she could try to surround her husband with love and affection, a wall so strong that there was no crevice through which the devious ones could crawl. Celibacy was a very difficult life for a man who must daily mix with the bawdy frontier life of America.

Mrs. Edwards realized that Esther's problems, although basically different from her own, would still be sufficiently similar. Civilization and pioneer life both possessed the same undercurrents. Although the methods employed would vary from sophistication to primitivism, one did not escape problems by retreat to a different culture. Mr. Burr, unlike the young Mr. Edwards, was no young defenseless minister. He was an experienced bachelor. Age and experience had made him deft in his own self-protection. Yet now that he wanted to marry it would not be wise to delay the wedding. It could be, the mother thought romantically, that Mr. Burr had always been in love with Esther and had merely waited for her to grow up. On the other hand, the practical thought intruded, there may have been some basic reason why his new appointment to the College of New Jersey called for a helpmate. If Esther dallied now, another less reluctant could take her place. And since Esther was in love with Mr. Burr, Mrs. Edwards had encouraged her daughter to follow her heart; and when Mr. Burr had, to everyone's surprise, urged an early wedding date, she had further encouraged her daughter to follow her heart, and helped her to feel her decision was right.

As they rode along together, the mother reminisced about her own early days as a bride. And, sensing her daughter's feeling of guilt at leaving the frontier, she erased for her any reluctance when her heart by preference urged her to a life of culture. It was God's way to appoint the meeting of a woman and her mate. Thereafter, wherever in life the providence of the Almighty led a man to his life work, woman followed. In this case she knew there was no reluctance on her daughter's part to leave the frontier, and she eased her daughter's conscience by pointing out this fact. She also stressed the great service which she could render to God in a citadel of culture. To each it was to serve in his appointed place.

It was a trip that mother and daughter never forgot. So often, with so many children about her, Sarah had regretted the inability to become intimate with each and every one of them as would have been possible with a smaller brood. The older ones were often most neglected for she had not the time to share each budding dream. She had only been able to be a home, a stable rock on which to lean in times of crisis. Her children grew up independent, secure, and loved. But on this trip to New Jersey, Sarah was glad for the chance for privacy and intimacy with this lovely girl, the daughter her husband felt was most like her.

34

Betty was the fragile member of the family. She had been born with a heart defect. Every minor disease was a serious one for her. Having this frail little sister always reminded the Edwards family, if they needed a reminder, that all flesh is like the grass. Betty was a delicate flower of the field serving in her sickness to underline the fact for them that all were mortal, and that it behooved each one to live under the aspect of eternity.

In Father's voluminous correspondence there would often be tucked a small note about Betty, who was ever on his mind. "Betty don't seem of late to be so well as she was in the summer. If she lives till spring I believe we must be obliged to come again to the use of the cold bath with her."

The children were always very solicitous of Betty. Whenever they were away their letters were full of affectionate greetings for this little sister. On their return they always sought her out as if to reassure themselves that she was still with them.

Always careful of contagious diseases, because of Betty they were even more cautious. On one occasion while in Northampton, Jonathan Edwards had refused to conduct evangelistic meetings in a

181

neighboring village because of the prevalence of measles in that place. His wife being pregnant at the time, he wrote regretfully that he deemed it unwise to expose himself and his wife to the disease since she was with child.

David Brainerd, in the last stages of tuberculosis, had been cared for by them in their home. But in those days tuberculosis had been an undiagnosed disease, and the threat of infection had not been known. They had not realized the danger to Jerusha, their daughter, who had for nineteen weeks, day and night, nursed the sick, tubercular man. Even while emotionally involved with the tragic death of David Brainerd, Jonathan Edwards had not lost his academic interest in the progress of the illness. He charted it in detail, as impersonal as a physician. Today his record is so clear that any modern doctor would immediately recognize the disease.

There was no shrinking back from any unpleasantness associated with the care of the dying man. If Jonathan Edwards had been aware of the danger of exposure to his family, as he was in the case of diphtheria or measles, he may have counseled otherwise. As it was he insisted that this homeless missionary stay under his own roof spending his last days on earth surrounded by whatever comfort they could give him.

Jonathan Edwards was an early pioneer in his interest in disease prevention, an early exponent of immunization. Whenever he felt a course of action to be right, the medical profession found that he, a minister, felt he should lead the way.

Frail Betty was cared for meticulously. The family never needlessly exposed her to disease. In spite of their precautions she was bedfast the greater part of her life. The closest sisters in age, because of the demands made on the family by this fragile member, were by the very nature of the situation given less attention. Susannah, or "Sukey," as the family called her, had a happy, sunny disposition. She was outgoing and affectionate. Eunice, who was three years younger, was inclined to turn inwards and crawl more and more into her own private world. She was a quiet child who was content to sit and observe the others. She was easily overlooked and forgotten. When the children returned from berry-picking, frequently they were all the way home before someone missed Eunice.

Eunice preferred to play quietly by herself. She and Sukey, each in her own way, adjusted to an invalid sister. This little sister who spent so much time sick and confined to bed developed in the two older sisters, so different in outlook, a common profound pity for all weak and helpless creatures.

Sukey would find a baby bird fallen too early from the nest. It would be Eunice who then took over the task of mothering the baby fledgling. In winter it was these two sisters who fed the wild creatures, who put out salt for the deer and crumbs for the wild birds.

It pleased Jonathan Edwards to see his two children standing in the garden while the shy birds came boldly down to eat from their hands. It reminded him of his own sister Jerusha, who had always been known for her kindness "to the beasties."

Sukey would purse up her little mouth and make bird calls so realistic that they would be answered. But it was Eunice who sat so still that the squirrels would frolic in her lap.

Timothy was the logical child in the family. Even as a toddler, scarcely able to talk, when someone told Timothy, "If you wash your face that black spot will come off," he would immediately fix his penetrating eyes on the speaker and retort with, "And if I don't wash my face, the black spot will not come off."

He always wanted to have life sorted out in straight lines for himself. It was no surprise to the family when he chose law for a profession. They had been accustomed in the family to the mock trials sponsored by Timothy. Some little one would be designated the criminal and big brother Timothy would play the prosecutor. Usually Esther would plead the case of the defendant. Even Venus and Rose would be pressed into jury duty.

When Father spoke he was apt to look steadily in one spot. His son had all the tactics of a lawyer. He would sweep the jury with his eyes, fixing his attention on Rose or one of the gentler jurymen who he knew had a soft spot in her heart for the trembling prisoner in the dock, and whose crime, that of robbing the cookie jar, struck a chord of sympathy.

The children missed their brother who was away in school. His visits, with all the drama that they entailed, were eagerly anticipated. Jonathan, especially, was glad to relinquish his role of the oldest son in his family of sisters.

With Mary, Sarah, and now Esther gone, it was good for them all to feel that their student brother Timothy was still theirs, only loaned by them to the College of New Jersey for a time.

35

"Move!" said the African woman with her mouth full of pins.

Lucy stood on a footstool dressed only in chemise and flared petticoat. The petticoat was made of yellow satin filled with a layer of cotton wadding and quilted in place. In the backwoods it was seldom that the more fashionable hoop skirt was worn; it was more practical even for dress occasions to wear the quilted underskirt. It puffed out at her tiny waist calling attention to that beauty target of the period.

While Lucy turned, Venus gently placed the overdress in place and busied herself pinning up its hem. It was made of yellow and white striped chintz. Most of the time it would be looped up to avoid contact with the dusty roads. But at the moment Venus wanted to be sure that when it did hang down it would not be uneven.

Mother arranged about the young girl's neck a dainty white muslin fichu. On her head she slipped the little white cap made of the finest gauze trimmed in lace, which Lucy herself had made. The child looked, standing on the stool, like a Yankee version of the Dresden shepherdess. Only unlike

the statue Lucy could not stand still. She was the
most impatient of all the girls. Even her own tiny
quilting stitches in the petticoat showed her impa-
tience with any demanding painstaking work. But
she had finally reached that strange threshold into
womanhood when suddenly the little girl who a
day before had cared not a whit for clothes would
endure and stand and primp and fuss over a hem
the slightest fraction out of line. This metamorpho-
sis was nothing new to Venus. She had gone
through it with all the Edwards girls. Now it was
Lucy's turn. She paid it scant respect. Her attitude
toward these teen years was: "This too shall pass."

It was Mrs. Edwards who stood back saddened in
the melancholy manner of all mothers to realize
that yet another fledgling was about to leave the
nest. She regretted yet rejoiced to see the first awk-
ward movement of flight on untried wings. Lucy
was in the magic borderland between youth and
adulthood.

"Mother, may I borrow your shawl tonight?"
This was the large wrap, a favorite of all the girls,
which Mother wore on cold winter evenings. It had
been a part of the dowry she had brought with her
when she married Mr. Edwards. It was made of soft
Kashmiri wool skillfully embroidered, an heirloom
which she in turn had received from her mother. It
became in the Edwards family a symbol of young
womanhood. When one of her girls began to borrow Mother's shawl, she had closed the door firmly

on girlhood.

Lucy had grown up the quickest of her daughters. Pioneer life had a way of ripening girls at an early age. Sarah Edwards analyzed this child of hers. She had Esther's quick wit, but combined with it a trace of the stolidness of her oldest daughter Sarah, a stubbornness lacking in the other girls. Lucy had always been extremely dependable, and often, when very young, had tackled and done well a task which would have held back a more timid child. There was never any of the hesitancy or shyness of Jerusha about this young lady. And now she too had entered upon these wonderful bewildering years, these mirror-conscious days when the unself-conscious beauty would become a conscious one. How well she, the mother, managed to help with the transition would determine the future of her daughter. Mother, busy as she was, realized she must allow more time for Lucy. The girl would be retreating within herself unless at these crucial moments she could be assured that there was always an open line to her. Any semblance of a closed door she would seize upon as an excuse to augment her own new, instinctive desire to withdraw from the world of adult advice and adult counsel. Her happy girl would become sad for no reason. Father once again would ask bewilderedly in the way of men, "What has happened to Lucy?" Mother would reassure him. The words of the verse applied to this daughter so well. It could have been written for Lucy:

> A child
> But yesterday.
> A woman tomorrow.
> Today she walks the vale of tears
> And teens.

36

Sarah Parsons sat and rocked by her fire. From the window she watched Elihu chop up the heavy logs in the yard. The miracle of being his wife she wrapped about her like a shawl. How well she remembered the day when all her own hopes toward this goal of hers had lain in ruins about her. Every detail of that morning remained scarred in her memory.

Snow, the first of the winter, had been blowing softly through the open casement. She had slipped out of bed to shut the window. In spite of her caution her sister Jerusha had awakened and sat up in bed. Jerusha seemed to sleep on the border of waking at all times, and when that frail barrier collapsed she awakened at once, all in one piece, as it were, physically and mentally alert. Sarah loved to lie in bed in that in-between state, feeling each bone in her body arouse leisurely to another day. She hated to get out of the tunnel of warmth which her feather bed afforded her. She was reluctant to feel the first thrust of the cold wooden floor against her warm bare feet. She never, like Jerusha, could rush out to meet each new day as if it were her last. And today of all days she wanted to believe that if she stayed in bed longer time would slow down and the private hour which had been scheduled with her father would be delayed.

Jerusha had finished dressing and Sarah was still in bed when the booming voice of Venus came up the stairwell: "Breakfast in five minutes."

"Do not make Father angry by being late on this day of your private time with him," her sister pleaded.

"Does it matter any more today than any other day?" retorted Sarah. His children were all aware that their father's memory was phenomenal. He was quite capable of remembering a tardy arrival at a meal even if it had occurred a fortnight before the scheduled date of giving account.

Jerusha looked worried. She came over and sat on the edge of the counterpane. "Sarah, I am sorry for you. I know how very much you love Elihu. But in a way, too, I am glad. How selfish I am. But I do not want you to marry first. I do not want to lie alone and look at your empty bed."

Sarah threw a pillow at her only to miss and hit Mary who had put her head in the door.

Mary returned the pillow with a deadly aim. "Hurry, Sarah, or you will be late again."

"You'd best not wait, Mary. Go on down," Jerusha counseled, "I will wait for Sarah." She rushed around the room helping the late one dress to make the deadline. With both cooperating they managed to race down the corridor and with a quick change of gait walk sedately arm in arm down the curving stairway in time for breakfast. Sarah triumphantly, behind her hand, made a face at Mary.

When all were in their places Father said grace and, excusing himself, left the family to retire to his study. He frequently spent thirteen hours a day studying. He managed this amazing amount of time by husbanding every hour of the day. He usually arose at four in the morning, indulging himself in the later rising time of five in the winter. In this way he was far along in his studies while the household still slept. He preferred to eat alone, usually certain foods which he had by experimentation discovered kept his mind and body most sprightly. This morning he did not eat the rich menu which Venus set before the rest of the household, the home-cured bacon and the delicious hot breads. But at the end of the meal he rejoined his family for morning devotions. In this way while his wife and children ate he had saved an hour of this most precious commodity for himself, time.

Usually the hour spent as a family with God began with a song. The Edwards children all had good voices. Father would use the tuning fork, and together they would sing their favorite songs of praises. Venus would supply her own variation of harmony in her rich contralto voice. In her own way, listening to beat and measures not heard by

Puritan ears, she lent a pulsating obbligato of primitive beauty. The children all loved to hear Venus sing. The youngest had all been crooned to sleep by her songs. They associated her songs with peace, tranquility and security.

Sarah Parsons always thought of these times with God in the morning in the words that her father had used in one of his letters, "Having found him, who is as the appletree among the trees of the wood, we may sit under his shadow with great delight, and his fruit will be sweet to our taste."

After breakfast they would all go their separate ways. Father would go back to his study, the older girls to their assigned household chores, the younger children to their studies. But they all knew that, at the end of the day, their father would rejoin them. It was his custom every evening to allow himself a season of relaxation in the midst of his family.

Father spent the morning in his study. He visited the sick in his parish only when they asked for him. And instead of house-to-house visitation of his parish he would preach frequently at private meetings in particular neighborhoods, establishing an early colonial pattern of the cottage prayer meeting.

Children of his flock would be invited to his own home for a time of catechism and prayer. He was very sure that the catechetical method of question and answer was a fine method of instruction. It prevented any padding of answers and confined the child to answering to the point. His questions were of the type that elicited from the child short answers, a type of oral completion test. The answer given must be not only accurate but concise.

Father's concern for time was often misunderstood. Other pastors were more social. He himself felt that his own talent did not lie in the realm of casual conversation, and he acknowledged he was inept in this art. He could not seem to lead the conversation easily into religious channels in the drawing room. He preferred, because of his own limitations, to have those who wanted answers to seek him outside of a social context. He was always available to all who wanted this contact, young and old, and even to his own children. They soon learned they should not bother Father needlessly, but if they did have problems they never hesitated to run with them to him.

Mrs. Edwards usually handled minor problems and disciplines. Today, however, daughter Sarah had been scheduled to meet with him, because Mother felt in Sarah a brooding resentment toward her father and believed it could be handled best by a private time with him.

He was writing in his journal when at the stroke of ten his wife and daughter entered the study. Mr. Edwards faithfully recorded in his diary all the events of his life, often so detachedly that his wife wondered if he looked on his own vicissitudes as an observer.

She thought as she entered of the young poet of England, Oliver Goldsmith, whose works, together with *Pamela*, the latest work of Richardson, Mrs. Erskine had recently sent her. Some lines of his poem "Deserted Village" describing the village parson of Auburn came to her as she looked at her husband:

As some tall cliff, that lifts its awful form,
Swells from the vale, and midway leaves the
*   storm,*
Though round its breast the rolling clouds are
*   spread,*
Eternal sunshine settles on its head.

Mr. Edwards stood as the women entered, and when his wife indicated her preference to be absent from the interview he selected for his daughter a chair in which to sit. He looked at her affectionately. Esther always reminded him most of his wife. But of all his children this one reminded him most of himself.

Mr. Edwards loved her. She was not tactful. She lacked many a desirable feminine virtue. But she was made of rock, this oldest child of his, and she had a fine clear masculine mind.

He laid his hand over her own. "Sarah, this I want to tell you. I felt honesty made it necessary for me to warn your suitor of your disposition, but if I had been in his place my own comments would not have deterred me. I would have felt your other good traits compensated for your temperament. I would have married you no matter what your own father had cautioned me about."

"Thank you, Father. Thank you very much."

In his own way Father had been a prophet. Elihu Parsons had not been scared away. He had doggedly continued to court this oldest daughter of Jonathan Edwards, and in the end wed her with her father's blessing.

37

Sarah Parsons shook a rug outside the casement window. As she leaned out she saw her sister Lucy disappearing into the woods with Jahreel Woodbridge. Both had ice skates slung carelessly over their shoulders. They appeared to be headed for the Mill Pond near his home.

Sarah looked displeased. Jahreel, although younger than Lucy, was a towering giant of a boy. Lucy herself had grown much older in experience than her years would indicate in this pioneer outpost. She had no opportunity in Stockbridge to meet many young men whom Sarah would consider eligible. It looked as if, because Jahreel was the best the wilderness had to offer, Lucy was going to gravitate toward him. Sarah hated to see Lucy marry just anyone.

Esther had waited and married suitably a man whose station in life was already established; but young Lucy scarcely remembered friends in Northampton and as she did not, like Esther, have memories to halt her it looked as if the situation in Stockbridge was weighted heavily in Jahreel's favor. He was full of strength and vigor, an excellent athlete, excelling in sports that would dazzle any young girl. And there was no doubt of how he felt toward Lucy.

As she went about dusting her log cabin Sarah thought, with a twinge of envy, of the beautiful home of Aaron Burr, where her sister was mistress. Every letter from Esther was full of its descriptions. Elihu had spent love and care making their wilderness home comfortable. She was proud of her husband. He was good and strong and extremely kind. And he loved her, she never forgot that, enough to set himself even against her own father in marrying her. He let her have her own way. Yet oddly, in the end, she did not want Lucy to marry a man like him. She coveted for her sister a man who could match her own brilliant wit, and not a plodder like Jahreel.

She took some mending out of the basket and as she rocked, watching her children at play, she darned a sock meticulously. Her darning, like that of all the Edwards girls, was a work of art. It pleased her to do these tasks. She had chosen this life. Her husband had come to Stockbridge because of her. There were the occasional moments of envy for Esther's way of life, but for herself she felt she had chosen well.

But Lucy. She had more ambitions for her sister than for herself. She had few illusions about her own personality. Honesty was her strongest characteristic. She was the oldest sister, and she knew she was often bossy and curt with those she loved.

Elihu was a saint. He put up with her and loved her
in spite of herself. They were well suited. She had
made a good match. But this Jahreel Woodbridge
was all muscle, too young and too immature and
too unestablished. Such a marriage involved a risk.
It hurt Sarah to see Lucy who could have somebody settle for anybody.

It was as well that Sarah possessed a wry sense of
humor, inherited from her father. Lucy did marry,
against her sister's wishes, Jahreel Woodbridge.
And the young man proved her predictions wrong.
He emerged in history to become a cultured and capable gentleman, far removed from the back-
woodsman Sarah Parsons had imagined, and
served his country honorably as a state senator. In
spite of her sister Sarah, little Lucy did marry a
somebody.

38

It was the birth of the foal that had reminded Sarah Edwards so poignantly of her daughter Jerusha. She, like Sukey and Eunice, had a way with the timid creatures of the woods. How she would have loved Stockbridge! How she had yearned to be a wilderness bride!

Thoughts of her dead daughter prevented sleep, and when she fell into a measure of subconsciousness she found herself living again in the past. She stood in her daughter's room helping her pack her few necessities. David Brainerd, Jerusha's fiance, had been visiting them, and had fallen to hemorrhaging severely. It seemed imperative that he be sent to seek a physician's help in Boston. Jerusha, usually so tractable, was insisting on riding with him.

"Mother, if David dies . . ."

The voice was so real. Like a spectator she saw herself. She even heard her own answer, "If David dies, my darling, it will be God's will, and you will take it as such."

Once again she heard the prophetic words, "I couldn't live without him."

This was a scene she relived many times in the

land which lay between waking and sleeping. As always the same alarm gripped her. Girls for generations had said such things and gone on to marry and produce large pioneer families in happiness. But there was a quality in Jerusha she had always felt, an otherworldliness, that made her catch her breath.

Maybe this was why her husband had given his consent to his daughter and made it possible for her to go along as David's traveling companion. It was a long journey for a young unmarried couple to make; but when she had questioned her husband's decision he had merely raised his eyebrows.

"One can only do what is right. I do not relish breaking social conventions, Mrs. Edwards. They are society's rules which serve as useful hedges. But this situation is unique and warrants their breaking. David will not live if he does not get medical help immediately. Jerusha is a good nurse. She is not only able and fit to travel with him, but is frantic to do so. No one could be better with him. And the very presence of his betrothed will sustain him. Conventions are not made by God but by man, and in this instance when we may save a life by breaking them, and such a valuable life, there is no hesitation on my part to give the couple my permission and my blessing."

The anxious Edwards family had gathered on the large veranda in Northampton and watched while the slaves had carried David to the body of the coach. They had tucked the warm robes about him. Jerusha, with her collar tucked up high under her chin, and her small face half obscured by the soft wool bonnet, climbed in beside him. She was already fussing with his covers as the coach pulled away. When David was with her she seemed to be totally oblivious to everyone. It was David, weak as he was, who waved.

"Will David die, Father?" young Jonathan asked fearfully.

Jonathan Edwards winced at the question. "That is as God wills."

"I do not want David to die. I love David."

Jonathan Edwards took his little boy in his arms and comforted him. Turning to Sarah, he said softly, "David is so well named. He has that rare quality so few men possess, that of the well beloved. He is like the David in the Bible. All love him for, like his Saviour, he is love."

Sarah watched him set his young son down tenderly. There was no roughness in her husband. She knew as he was speaking of David that he was comparing him to himself. Her husband, someone had said, was all mind, a machine, a keen intellect with no heart. Seeing his gentleness with his son she resented the comparison. She knew the depths of emotion her husband possessed. But unlike David Brainerd, Jonathan Edwards's heart was not transparent. David would make more friends in life. Her husband, she felt, would influence more lives in his own generation and the next. And she was content.

She knew what this moment meant to him. It was he, as much as his young son, who needed comforting. She slipped her arm through his as they stood watching the empty road to Boston. "I am glad we let Jerusha go with him."

"Jerusha!" She was restless. Most of her words, like most sleep-talking, were unintelligible. But her husband heard his daughter's name plainly and sensed she was reliving the loss of the one who had been so dear to them both. He laid his long hand gently over her own. She clenched it fiercely for a moment, then relaxed in slumber.

39

Sarah was not the only one who mourned Jerusha. As always happens in large families, especially if the eldest are girls, the little ones fall to the special care of one of the older sisters. These little mothers help to give all the care and cuddling which the busy mothers are too often unable to offer. For Esther Edwards it was young Susannah, or "Sukey," as they affectionately dubbed her, who was her charge. Lucy, scarcely grown up herself, nevertheless took on the role of mother protector to baby Pierrepont. Jonathan's little mother had been Jerusha. He had been only a toddler when she died. An adult would have felt he was too young to remember. Only his mother sensed that this little boy of hers hurt with a secret ache the dead sister had left him in legacy.

Mother was a violin which responded to the slightest touch. She had that choice combination of intelligence and extreme sensitivity. Busy as she was, she gave her young son every moment she could spare for him.

The doctor, early in her marriage, had ordered that Sarah Edwards devote some time each day to riding. It was his view that the fresh air and exercise

were therapeutic for her. There was nothing so ex-
hilarating for the weary mother as to sit astride a
beloved horse and, at one with the mount, to gallop
off into the Berkshires. Her young son, Jonathan,
the best rider of her children, often went with her.
They would ride silently, seldom speaking much,
joined in a spirit in awe as they rode or reined in
their mounts at a favorite spot of beauty. It was this
that Jonathan wanted—not the vivacious teasing of
Esther or Lucy—but this immense quiet, this loving
stillness of his mother. Her husband had often remarked about this quality in his wife, a wordless
communion achieved with another creature.
Mother unconsciously exerted her charm on all she
met. She always stirred in the opposite sex admiration and an awareness of her femininity. She had
that quality of making a man awake to the fact that
she was different, a creature of gossamer substance
against which his own masculinity became more
apparent, and which caused him to lift his shoulders and even to strut a little.

Her daughter Esther inherited this quality from
her mother, but Esther turned the gift into flirtation
and sauciness. She deliberately used it. But her
mother restrained the gift, appeared unaware of it,
and with her great devotion to God so uppermost
in her heart this quality became obscured. Yet her
saintliness did not dim her extreme attractiveness
to those who met her. Although it was not
flaunted, many, even those who were not of her

own religious persuasion, remarked about her charm.

Even her young son was not immune to this femininity of his mother. He never forgot when he rode with her that she was a woman and that he was her protector. He became a little man. She brought out every quality of manhood in him. And even while her eyes were alert to the dangers of the forest she indulged and encouraged this strength in him and let him feel it was he upon whom their safety rested. It was good, she felt, for Jonathan to strut a little.

40

It was a rainy fall day. Even the luster of the scarlet maples was diluted by the dullness of the haze which hung over the mountains.

Sarah Edwards went up to the garret to do some spinning. She could hear Pierrepont, who was beginning to use his ten-word vocabulary with great efficiency, talking with Venus. It always had amazed her, the courtesy with which the slaves listened to children. They treated every observation of theirs with weighty consideration as if there was something very special in the world only children could know and only a wise adult could learn second-hand—if he listened.

It was always possible to know the exact whereabouts of Pierrepont Edwards. Unlike her other children, he had always been exceedingly vocal in his demands. He, the family agreed, was a child who had never learned to whisper.

Sarah enjoyed spinning. It was the most creative of her household duties. She was awed to see a length of thread become, under her skillful maneuver, cloth out of which she could keep her family warm.

As she worked the treadle she heard the lumbering footsteps on the stairs. It could only be Pierrepont seeking her. This youngest child was at the tenacious age. He wanted to stay as close to her as possible. If Mother were out of sight for even a minute the secure world of Pierrepont Edwards collapsed. She smiled at him as he entered—a welcome he evidently expected. As always he responded with a cherubic grin. Even as a babe in arms when someone patted Pierrepont on the back, he would gently thump the person's back in return with his baby fist. If anyone ruffled his hair he reached up and tugged the instigator's in return. Responsive Pierrepont!

After he had sat on her lap long enough to gain back his aggressive self-assertiveness, he climbed down and ferreted out his rocking horse from the corner store of toys. The advantage of a big family was the accumulation of playthings the youngest received. This horse's face came straight out of mythology. It was chipped and battered, a true antique, but it still rocked. It had come along, an essential item, with the wagon of goods to Stockbridge.

Pierrepont rocked and Mother spun. The noise of the spinning wheel combined with the rocking motion of the horse caused the little rider to droop. Mother put away her work, gently picked him up and carried him downstairs for his nap. He had a large baby bed on rockers. All of her children had insisted on squeezing into this bed as long as they could. She had soothed them all with its rocking motion. Now as little Pierrepont tried to unstick his eyelids she rocked his bed gently and softly sang a lullaby.

Venus thumped up the stairs, "I didn't mean for him to bother you."

Sarah smiled. "It makes me feel sad to think he may be the last baby I can fondle."

Venus, practical as always, grunted her relief that her mistress had ended her days of child-bearing. But Sarah Edwards had caught the old slave cuddling Pierrepont much more even than the other children, and she realized that they were both enjoying their twilight of motherhood.

41

They had been living in Stockbridge two years when Mrs. Edwards became very ill. Her husband wrote to a friend in Scotland on her recovery that "My wife has been very dangerously sick, so as to be brought to the very brink of the grave. . . . But God was pleased to preserve her, and mercifully to restore her to a pretty good state of health."

Mother's sickness had been a severe blow to the children. The family by now was accustomed to the frailness of little Betty. Every illness she suffered made them face frankly the fact that God might call upon them to relinquish this young life they loved so dearly. Even Father's ill health the children faced stoically, for his health had always been in a precarious state; but mother had always seemed indestructible. It shook their sense of security to realize that she too was mortal. They tiptoed downcast about the home. Father's face was drawn. He did not try to ease their worry, for he did not hide the fact from them that their mother was facing eternity, and he reassured them only with the comfort of the fact that she possessed an "unweaned resignation to the Divine will." How much lighter the air seemed when her gentle hands again resumed the reins.

Then from July 1753 to January 1754, Father, so frequently buffeted by illness, became gravely ill. Never very heavy, his flesh fell away leaving him a gaunt skeleton. He shook so with the fever chills that he could scarcely hold a pen. His recovery again was followed by a prolonged convalescence which left him helplessly weak. This especially fretted the industrious man who budgeted his time so carefully. In one of the first letters he felt able to write he confided to his friend, Mr. Erskine in Scotland, that this was the "most tedious illness that ever I had in life."

Because there was so much sickness about, and because he was by nature always curious about every field of science, Jonathan Edwards followed each advance in medicine with an interest unusual for a layman. He frequently recorded not only prescriptions, but his own opinions of them.

In the family prescription chest was a favorite family remedy: "Take mustard seed bruised and steeped in wine, and the wine [should be] taken three or four spoonfuls two or three times a day."

But although the family quickly availed themselves of the best medical advice of the day, they never forgot for a moment the dispenser of health and the withholder of the same. In every sickness the children were taught to resign themselves to the will of God.

Father's letters to his children abounded in

physical, but especially spiritual admonitions. His prescription was best expressed in a letter he had written to young Mary who was away visiting an aunt in Portsmouth:

My Dear Child,

You may think it is natural for a parent to be concerned for a child at so great a distance, so far out of the reach of communication; where, if you should be taken with any dangerous sickness, that should issue in death, you might probably be in your grave before we could hear of your danger. But yet, my greatest concern is not for your health, or temporal welfare, but for the good of your soul. Though you are at so great a distance from us, yet God is every-where. You are much out of the reach of our care, but you are every moment in His hands. We have not the comfort of seeing you, but He sees you. His eye is always upon you. And if you may but live sensibly near to God, and have his gracious presence, it is no matter if you are far distant from us. I had rather you should remain hundreds of miles dis-tant from us, and have God near to you by his Spirit, than to have you always with us, and live at a distance from God. And if the next news we should hear of you should be of your death, though that would be very melancholy; yet, if at the same time we should receive such intelligence concerning you, as should give us the best grounds to hope that you had died in the Lord, how much more comfortable would this be, though we should have no opportunity to see you, or take leave of you in your sickness, than if we should be with you during all its progress, and have much opportunity to attend upon you, and converse and pray with you, and take an affectionate leave of you, and after all have reason to apprehend, that you died without the grace and favor of God! It is comfortable to have the presence of earthly friends, especially in sickness, and on a death-bed; but the great thing is to have God our friend, and to be united to Christ, who can never die any more, and from whom our own death cannot separate us."

42

Once again with no warning the ague struck down Jonathan Edwards. For seven days he ran a high temperature. During the night following the familiar chills started. The high fever was breaking at last, but the extreme drop in temperature was too rapid for his body to adjust to safely. He shook with chills, so severe that the very bed shook with him.

Sarah piled on blankets to warm her husband, to try to stop his chattering teeth. She rushed to get more bed warmers. The chills ended as abruptly as they had begun leaving her husband too weak to care. She forced some hot broth between his clenched lips and relaxed only when she noticed that he had fallen into an uneasy slumber.

She lay beside him grateful but exhausted. Some night, she always feared, the chills would not abate in time and the weakened man would die. Jonathan Edwards had always been frail. There were few in this rugged country with a constitution like her husband's who had survived so long. Pioneer life in the wilderness weeded out the sick and infirmed in infancy. Seldom did the weak live until maturity. But Jonathan Edwards had been spared. It was almost as if he had not been permitted to succumb. After a family of eleven girls, Timothy and Esther Stoddard Edwards had their son at last. They would keep him, with God's help. Watchful care by the parents, aided willingly by eleven sisters, had enabled the sickly boy to reach a delicate manhood. At marriage Sarah Pierrepont Edwards had inherited the task of fanning the health of Jonathan Edwards. It was she who must keep the flickering flame alive through the frequent bouts with the wasting fever. They had tried every known medicine for the ague. She only hoped the Peruvian bark the doctor had promised to send would be more effective.

The chief worry about the disease was its weakening symptom. Even the great intellect of her husband, and the equally great will, seemed unable to survive this debilitation. Jonathan Edwards seemed unable after these bouts of ill health to exert the slightest effort of will, not enough to lift a hand to paper, or even to summon any thought another could record.

"Mrs. Edwards."

She turned to face him. "I thought you were asleep."

"If I should die, how would you manage?"

Sarah Edwards thought of the various penuries the family was practicing at the moment—the fans they made which Sally Prince was selling for them on the Boston market to amplify her husband's salary. Now if that salary should cease . . .

"The Lord will provide." She adjusted the blankets about him. "You are not to worry."

Her husband smiled wanly. It was not the practical answer he expected from this wife of his who ran her household so well on so little.

"Through whom and by what means? Our finances are at a low ebb. The house in Northampton is not yet sold."

"It will be in time. You must not be concerned for us." She wiped the sweat from his face. "And Elihu will help."

"Yes. Elihu is always eager to do what he can, but already he has his own large family and his resources are totally taxed with their own needs. No," he said reluctantly, "It will have to be Timothy who takes the load. Timothy is a good manager, and he will not shirk his duty. He will do it well. He has almost finished school. I shall speak to him about assuming the duties of the head of this home in the eventuality it should become necessary.

"Timothy will . . ." Her husband, satisfied, drifted away again into an uneasy sleep.

43

Venus wore her bandanna wrapped like a turban about her tight gray curls. Her skirt was always voluminous. This latest she was wearing was a splendid creation made from Indian madras. She never seemed to become kitchen-splattered. Her apron remained dazzling white. How she managed to fry her delicacies on her iron skillet, usually not over the coals but adjacent to them in order to get reflected heat, and yet avoid the spattering grease, was her own culinary secret. By contrast, Rose always emerged looking slightly soiled. This good-looking slave had a mania for clean hands, but consequently her apron corners were grimy for she had the habit of wiping her hands upon it. The immaculate Venus barely tolerated her in her domain, and she usually spent her day busy making beds or in other less greasy chores. The kitchen was Venus' kingdom. It was hers by length of service. Even Mrs. Edwards did not question her dictates within its walls.

Venus hoped that Jonathan would come back with a promised squirrel. He was the best hunter in the family. He could shoot squirrel by "barking" them. That is, instead of blasting the small game to bits he would hit a tree immediately beside it so that the animal would be killed by the blast and not the shot. The squirrels Jonathan brought home she could be sure would not be blown to bits.

It was pleasant to vary the family diet by fresh game. Venus was a good cook and especially proud of her johnnycakes. She made these out of thin batter with sour milk, soda, salt, and whatever shortening she had on hand. She made them dry, as good johnnycakes should be. Actually the cakes were originally called journey cakes, and they were made dry so that they would last as rations for travelers. She liked to set a good table and it was pleasant to be able to vary the diet with fresh game during migrating season with duck or goose or pigeon. Today she would be lucky to get a squirrel. But it would make a good pot pie. Her pot pies were a stew with dumplings, especially fine, she felt, reheated the next day. She always felt it a tragedy when she had to fall back on turnips or her stable, corn meal mush. She went around with a long face when the cow was dry and this mush could not be moistened with rich milk and she had to substitute maple syrup. This was truly the bottom of her barrel.

One thing Venus had to say for her family: they never complained. The master said the same gracious thanks over the poorest of her meals as over her best; but it made Venus sad to see such eloquence of grace wasted and she always felt she had

been guilty of letting down Mr. Edwards and the
Almighty in that order. Thanks to Jonathan this did
not occur too often, for they made a good team, he
the hunter and she the cook, and she was heard to
brag in glum moments to Rose, to boost her own
spirits, that very few visitors found fault with her
victuals. That was an African Puritan's understatement.

44

On August 17, 1756, Esther Burr, now three years married, surprised her family and Stockbridge almost "out of their wits" by a visit. She brought with her little Sally, who was two years of age, and baby Aaron, a chubby child of six months.

Little Sukey, especially, was ecstatic. She and Eunice now had something special to mother, a little baby all their own.

All the family kept journals. They painstakingly stitched sheets of paper together to make these diary books. Esther wrote in hers diligently from October 1, 1754 to September 2, 1757. Speaking of her visit home that autumn she wrote, "A very busy day with us for my brother sets out for the Jerseys on Monday. And on Tuesday my Mother sets out for Northampton, my sister Dwight is near her time so I never said one word against it although I am come 150 miles to see my friends and apt to think I shall not come again in many years if ever."

Esther was hurt. She wanted and needed this time with her parents. There were so many new ideas and problems she had met in Princeton, and she wanted to talk them over with her loved ones whose wisdom she had relied on so very much in the past. Surely Mother need not have gone to Northampton. She could have sent one of the girls. Esther was headstrong, and the fact that her unexpected visit should not upset already-laid plans of the family did not occur to her. She had made a long journey with a small baby, and instead of being treated like a conquering heroine she was immediately delegated to her role of one of the Edwards girls. The one whose need was the greatest was the one who received the attention.

After Mother left she wrote another entry in her private confessional that there was not "much added gloom" to her stay in Stockbridge. Father, however, gave her many precious hours of counseling. On the 19th of September she wrote this entry in her journal, "What a mercy that I have such a Father, such a Guide."

But the whole visit was made of nightmare proportions by the news which ironically Esther herself had been the first to break in Stockbridge, the disaster at Oswego.

In spite of French claims to the region in 1722, British and Dutch settlers had moved into the territory and a fort to support their rights had been built near the mouth of the Oswego River. Governor Burnet of New York, sensitive to the strategic value of the location, had paid the Five Nations for land on which to build. Unwilling to wait for the money to arrive through the channels of the penny-wise New York Assembly, and afraid of governmental delays, he had dug into his own purse to pay for the purchase. This completed fort was an insult to the French who controlled the Great Lakes and interrupted their otherwise comprehensive line of French fortifications. It had served the British well for it proved an effective barrier to any further French advancement into northern New York.

But in August, 1736 the Marquis de Montcalm had surprised the strategic fort of Oswego and captured it taking 1,600 prisoners. His undisciplined Red Indian allies had fallen upon his prisoners and butchered many before the French gentleman commander had finally been able to stop the massacre, only by appealing to the instinct of monetary gain, the amount of redemption money each prisoner represented. This was an all-time low for the British in the French and Indian wars in the Colonies. The news of the capture of Oswego tolled doom to the British town of Stockbridge, now even more defenseless in its unguarded wilderness. It was Esther herself who had been the harbinger of this bad news. Esther was frankly terrified of the Indians. She could not sleep. In her diary she recorded that she had not slept since she left New York. She added that "she wanted to be made willing to die in any way God pleases, but I am not willing to be butchered by a barbarous enemy."

The visit which she had anticipated with such animation was a dismal failure. The whole visit was doomed from the beginning by the terrifying Red Indian raids and the added indignation to her of the absence of her beloved mother. Her summation she wrote in her journal with her acid pen, "A most charming day. What a charming place this would be if it would not be for the inhabitants thereof."

45

Venus gave little Sally's curls an extra brushing. Her devotion to the Edwards family extended down to the next generation; in fact, it seemed it increased. Sarah Parsons's children were always assured of a cookie from the cookie jar—sometimes little Pierrepont Edwards was not. "It does not pay to spoil children" did not apply with her to the children not living under her own roof.

Esther lay back against her soft pillows and watched Venus work. Little Sally, femininity in a small package, sat primly with her ankles crossed while the negress brushed her hair. Today it was good to be home. There was always a feeling of serenity here. Outside the winds blew, but the family stayed calm. She was uneasy, however, even surrounded by this security for she realized that she had broken from this pattern. She had become more petulant with her own motherhood. She could not seem to take the buffetings of providence in the same sway-with-the-wind technique of her childhood. Father never seemed to get bitter even when he was deeply embroiled. He had let her read his diary which recorded his own dismissal from the Northampton charge. One would have thought the writer was talking of someone in the third person.

Now in Stockbridge with the Williams dispute there was never any blind rage on his part. She had said repeatedly "Ephraim Williams should be licked," but never in her father's presence.

This was one of the joys of coming home to talk things over with her father. She felt very close to him and so much easier in her mind when she had unloaded her problems on him. Her husband Aaron was too close to many of the new situations she faced to be able to help her. He often became amused by her seriousness over what he would consider a trifle. But Father had never laughed at any of her worries. Anything that troubled her was a serious matter to him.

Something whistled by the window. Esther sat up instantly alert "What was that?"

"Hush," reassured Venus, feeling the little girl tense. She peered out the side window. "It's only Jonathan practicing with his bow and arrow."

Esther settled back gingerly, the peace of the moment lost.

"How do you feel, Venus, about this unrest of the red men?"

"Just the way you does," the servant said shrewdly.

"One moment I want this visit to never end," confided Esther. "The next I can't wait to get back to civilization. Please don't tell Mr. Edwards, Venus. I would not dare to leave before the time of my visit ends. He would find me cowardly. Venus, when I go back, why not come with me? I know Mother would be happy to let you go for she knows you would be more comfortable and safe with us in New Jersey."

"No, child. That I could not do. My lot is the lot of the family. I just can't be a deserter. But I sure don't like the idea of my scalp hanging in some te-pee. I want it with me in my grave. I don't want the good Lord to have to find it is in some wigwam to get it for me come resurrection morning. I don't want Him to have to go to all that trouble connect-ing me up again. But you just take this little golden-haired angel home just as soon as you can. This is not the country for the likes of her. Don't you worry none about Mr. Edwards. I'll tend to him."

"I just don't dare leave early, Venus."

"I do declare, Miss Esther, I believe you are more afraid of your father than you are of the Indians."

"I reckon, Venus, I am."

The women giggled together. In her journal that evening Esther Edwards Burr wrote, "So I must tarry the propos'd time, and if the Indians get me, they get me."

46

Esther Edwards Burr was the girl who had everything: a husband she not only loved but admired, two lovely children, and a beautiful home. Her friends were the elite of New Haven. Even Governor Belcher was a frequent dinner guest. The only shadow over her life was the possibility that her pretty daughter Sally had inherited a touch of the wry neck which so beset the Edwards family. Her young son, Aaron, who had nearly died, had not only been fully restored to health but was growing up to be a grubby healthy typical boy. His mother could even complain complacently of him that he was a dirty little boy so unlike his immaculate sister Sally.

Then a series of calamities fell. Governor Belcher died. Her husband, President Aaron Burr, preached the funeral service. He had not been well all week running a very high fever, but he felt this gesture of friendship to the family of the one who had meant so much to the Christian cause in New England could not be refused. He left a sick bed to preach the funeral sermon only to return and collapse, his fever raging out of control. The world was shocked two days later to learn that Aaron Burr was dead.

Esther the lighthearted, vivacious wife died with him. She emerged chastened and devout, but an old woman. She took this tragedy, as she had been trained to do from infancy, as a frown from heaven. She wrote in anguish to her father, "Had not God supported me by these two considerations: first, by showing the right he has to his own creatures, to dispose of them when and in what manner he pleases; and secondly, by enabling me to follow him beyond the grave, into the eternal world, and there to view him in unspeakable glory and happiness, freed from all sin and sorrow; I should, long before this, have been sunk among the dead, and been covered with the clods of the valley—God has side ends in all that he doth. This thing did not come upon me by chance; and I rejoice that I am in the hands of such a God."

Her parents were grieved yet comforted by the correct manner in which their daughter was receiving this blow. By contrast their own life had been so peaceful. God had been good to them, for in all their travails together they had been spared each other. He had seen fit to bless the marriage of Aaron Burr and their daughter with only five short years. There seemed one practical way they could help. As soon as they heard the news Lucy began to pack her bags. The close-knit family knew how much comfort a sister could be at this time.

"Why, Mother?" asked her tearful daughter, "why did they have such a short time together?

Why did God take a man like Aaron Burr?"

"Let me read you, Lucy, what Esther herself says about the tragedy." She read slowly some precious excerpts from the letters which meant so much to her. Some she read from the one her husband received, but also from her own she chose to share this thought: "Heavenly and eternal things appear much more real and important than ever before. I feel myself to be under much greater obligations to be the Lord's than before this sore affliction."

Sarah Edwards could see in this tragedy—and it brought its own comfort—a deepening in the spiri tuality of one of her children. What she did not realize at the moment was how intertwined the tragedy of Aaron Burr was with her own in a more intimate degree. For it set the wheels in motion. Aaron Burr's death closed the chapter not only on his life, but on that of her own husband, Jonathan Edwards, missionary to the Stockbridge outpost.

For shortly there came a delegation of men who urged Jonathan Edwards to take upon himself the now vacant presidency of the College of New Jersey.

Mr. Edwards was most reluctant to accept the post. He felt himself to be most deficient in the Greek classics, in the New Testament, and, in addition, he felt that sickness had made him weak and not a man who had sufficient ease in conversation to hold this position which demanded, he felt, the suave touch of an Aaron Burr. Selfishly he could not help but feel that his life in Stockbridge had become a good one for a scholar. He could not deafen himself, however, to the cogent arguments of his friends. Finally being persuaded that the will of God for him lay in the new field of Princeton, Jonathan Edwards accepted the post. As was his way, he went on ahead to find a place in which to settle his "numerous family."

He left behind him a joyful, excited group. Jonathan was to ride down the path with his father. Mr. Edwards took leave of the others at his home. Turning to his wife and daughters he said, as usual, "I commit you to God." As Jonathan left his father at the fork in the road, the boy turned homeward without even a backward look. He was anticipating a joyful reunion as he raced his pony back to the stockade. His father reined his mount and watched the forest obliterate his young son. But he too had no premonitions of disaster.

Sarah Edwards had wept to see her husband leave. But in the privacy of her bedroom she often gave way to her grief, for she became increasingly distressed to see him set out on any long journey. This separation, she thought, was no different from any other. It was even easier for she anticipated life in New Jersey. Like her daughter Esther she was not overly fond of wilderness privations. But unlike Esther she had adapted well to them. She knew her husband was desirous for her sake too that they return to the city. As Jonathan Edwards rode alone this was one thought uppermost in his mind, how very well Sarah would fit into the new life. The thought teased across his mind that she would be happy anywhere with him. They had a rare and beautiful relationship, one which had begun in ecstasy and continued unabated through the years.

The girls were enthusiastic about the change. They especially anticipated their reunion with sister Esther. They were making plans how to transport their various pets along the wilderness road.

Jonathan, the most reluctant to leave, spent every precious moment with his friends the Housatonnucks. But his grief was assuaged knowing that soon he would be leaving for school anyway, and these halcyon days would end.

At this moment in history, medical science had taken a gigantic step forward; a new vaccine to prevent smallpox had been made. It had been tried successfully. This heralded event played its own grave part in the history of the Edwards family. Because the disease was prevalent in New Jersey, Jonathan Edwards, always at the forefront in his interest in medical research, volunteered to have himself vaccinated. He realized there was always risk with new revolutionary medical ideas, but he was impressed with the fact that the sister of Princess Sophie had been successfully vaccinated. The duty of the monarchy and the clergy was to lead if others were to follow. He, Esther Burr and her children were vaccinated.

Something went wrong. Jonathan Edwards soon

realized his condition, the significance of the pustules forming in his throat. With his usual clarity he knew he was dying. Unable to write, he called for Lucy who was caring for him and dictated to her a word of comfort to the one who had shared his life. Tell my "dear wife," he said, "that the uncommon union, which has so long subsisted between us, has been of such a nature, as I trust is spiritual, and therefore will continue for ever: and I hope she will be supported under so great a trial, and submit cheerfully to the will of God."

For the children also there was a tender word, for them "who are now like to be left fatherless; which I hope will be an inducement to you all, to seek a Father who will never fail you."

Shortly before his death, when it was thought he could speak no longer, he roused and said, "Trust in God, and ye need not fear."

Esther Burr, who had been vaccinated at the same time as her father, seemed to be well. Suddenly she too became very ill. Sixteen days later she died leaving two orphaned children. She was twenty-seven.

Only slowly by runner did the news of the double tragedy reach Stockbridge. They rallied from the one blow only to hear about the next.

On the death of her husband Sarah Edwards comforted the little ones about her. She took pen in hand to write to try to ease the pain, if she could, of the loved ones in New Jersey. To Esther Burr, the grieving widow, she wrote:

My Very Dear Child,

What shall I say? A holy and good God
has covered us with a dark cloud. O
that we may kiss the rod, and lay our
hands on our mouths! The Lord has
done it. He has made me adore his
goodness, that we had him so long.
But my God lives; and he has my
heart. O what a legacy my husband,
and your father, has left us! We are all
given to God; and there I am, and love
to be.

Your ever affectionate mother,
Sarah Edwards

The letter never reached Esther Burr. By the time
it arrived Esther Edwards Burr was dead.

In Stockbridge life went on. The bereaved
Edwards children had God and Mother.

47

Mother was returning from Boston with little Sally and Aaron Burr, Jonathan's cousins. There was never any question after they had been orphaned but that there would be room for them in Stockbridge. Ever since his father had died, it seemed any absence of his mother became twice as unbearable, and Jonathan eagerly looked forward to any news of her expected return. It was he who saw the runner and rushed to meet him at the gate. He had expected good news telling the time of the anticipated reunion. Instead it was Jonathan who first felt the blow. His beloved mother was never returning. She who had left them in such high courage had contracted dysentery on the way, and had simply not had the strength to throw off the wasting sickness. With none of her loved ones by her side she had released her hold on life. She had been in the ground for days and he had not known. Mother was dead.

It was Timothy who assumed the headship of the family, as his father had planned. Only a lad of twenty, he assumed without grumbling the full responsibility not only of the rearing of his three younger sisters and two brothers, but, in addition, he honored the last effort of his mother, and Sally and Aaron Burr became a part of his charge in the Stockbridge home.

The inheritance from his parents was slight. He received a slave of "mediocre value," a silver tankard valued at about sixty dollars, miscellaneous items including a porringer, and about one hundred and thirty-two dollars. The house was his. The library it contained was the most valuable item. It included three hundred and one volumes, five hundred and thirty-six pamphlets, forty-eight maps, thirty unpublished manuscripts, one thousand and seventy-four manuscript sermons—the total worth about four hundred and fifteen dollars. This library, as his father wished, was to go intact to any son who followed in his religious work. Honoring this wish, it was young Jonathan who ultimately received this legacy.

As for Timothy all aspiration to his own field of the law was now relinquished. Instead he became a wage earner—and a good one. But it was too exacting a way of life for such a young man. He could feed the mouths, but he could not manage the patient parenthood which he had received from his elders. He often was out of temper and spoke harshly to them. Jonathan, at thirteen, was able to understand this brother whom he admired so deeply, and could sympathize with his fits of anger. He appreciated all that his big brother was doing for him and the others, but he could not help but ache for the days when his mother had ruled them—she who never raised her voice or needed to raise a hand.

The pattern of life was changed. Mischievous Aaron Burr became progressively worse. His mother had written of her beloved boy, "He will need a firm hand." Remembering this, Timothy acted too severely on the advice. Aaron's last escapade had been climbing a cherry tree and throwing cherries at the spinster who had scolded him. For this prank he had been beaten most harshly. Even lovable Pierrepont was chafing at the harsh discipline unmitigated by love.

When Timothy married, at first it seemed the family situation could be saved and some of the old happy ways regained. His wife Rhoda was affectionate and kind. But soon she became a mother, and a succession of children kept her too busy to share herself enough with the older orphaned ones in her care. Timothy, with now even more effort needed to supply the physical wants of his family, became totally absorbed in this end. In material things Timothy Edwards prospered. His mercantile business became a great success, and his was the first real shop in the frontier town of Stockbridge.

But discipline without reasonableness and charity corroded the sensitive children. Aaron Burr became a perpetual truant from a house that was not a home. At last this brilliant son of stellar parents grew up to be an adult who was accused of playing truant even with his own country. A man who almost became President of the United States, the grandson of Jonathan Edwards and the son of Aaron Burr, he was tried for treason. If Aaron Burr's parents had lived, if even his grandmother, Sarah Pierrepont Edwards, had lived to rear him, would he still have cut his same sad meteorlike career across American history? It is interesting to note that after his acquittal from the charge of treason, and during the time of his disgrace, he made a short visit to the home of his uncle and aunt in Stockbridge. At that time his Aunt Rhoda remonstrated gently with him, telling him of her own unceasing prayers for him and reminding him of the legacy of his devout family. His answer was simply, "I hope to see them some day again in heaven."

Pierrepont, the baby, only eight when orphaned, departed from the Puritan tradition of his parents. Scarcely remembering their influence, he used his heritage of ability to become a prominent and successful man, but only in the things of this world.

Lucy married, as soon as possible, a man of whom her sisters disapproved, Jahleel Woodbridge. Little Betty, the cherished delicate child, died at thirteen. Only Eunice and Sukey, of the girls remaining, seemed to have achieved a normal, untwisted Christian growth.

Jonathan, with a bulwark of thirteen years with his own family, was not harmed. But he fled in his own way. He went away to grammar school as soon as possible and buried himself in his studies. He achieved brilliance in academic lines. At his first pastorate in New Haven, he met and fell in love with Mary Porter. His marriage with her recaptured for him all the sweetness and love he had known in his early youth. . .

Mother had whispered against his black hair while he held her horse for her to mount and set out on what was to be her last journey, "I will be back as soon as I can, my son." She had never returned.

He had told Mary this morning, "I will only be a moment." She had not lived to see him again.

The wind blew the canopy about his head. The fog of the past was clearing. His journey back into his childhood was ending. He saw clearly now what this pilgrimage was teaching him. He had been, as it were, an Indian papoose, a little Turkeylegs strapped securely to a cradle board, hanging safe in a crotch of the tree. The winds had blown and would blow; but this security childhood memories gave him would never be lost. He had grown up a child of God. His father's last words supported him: "Trust in God and ye need not fear!" Mother had written, "O what a legacy your father has left us."

Even now, walking through the valley of the shadow, longing for the touch of the absent beloved ones—Jerusha, Father, Mother, Esther, and now his own dear Mary—he could rise from the ashes and plod solidly onward. He could say with David, "I shall go to her. . . . She will not return to me."

He had four children, Mary's and his own little ones, to whom this legacy must be passed. "Man proposes. God disposes" . . . "The frowns of heaven" . . ." O what a legacy" . . . "The vinegar of life." Jonathan no longer felt the soft tulle blow across his face. "No-Cry Eagle" was asleep.

48

As a young man, the elder Jonathan Edwards had written his resolutions for life. Among them were the following:

> Resolved, never to DO, BE, OR SUFFER, anything, in soul or body, less or more, but what tends to the glory of God.

> Resolved, never to lose one moment of *time*; but improve it in the most profitable way I possibly can.

> Resolved, to live with all my might, while I do live.

> Resolved, never, henceforward, till I die, to act as if I were any way my own, but entirely and altogether God's.

That he was able to fulfill these aims, written with such high courage before he was of age, was shown by the tribute the world paid him after his death.

President Mark Hopkins phrased his eulogy in this way: "It may be questioned whether the world can furnish a more signal example of the results of solitary thought."

"His power of subtle argument, perhaps unmatched, certainly unsurpassed among men" was the witness of Sir James Mackintosh.

Yale University inscribed on one of its chapel windows the testimony that he was "a philosopher of sacred things who moves the admiration of the ages."

His own Princeton University, then the College of New Jersey, had written above his dust that he was "second to no mortal man."

But his tributes did not stop at his own threshold. His own family's high esteem for him was even more remarkable, coming from the ones who knew him best. Sarah, his wife, summed it up in her words to her daughter Esther, "O what a legacy my husband, and your father, has left us!"

From his descendants have come presidents for Yale, Princeton, Union, Hamilton, Amherst, the University of California, the University of Tennessee, the Litchfield Canon Law School, Columbia Law School and Andover Theological Seminary.

Of the generation that immediately followed, his own son, Jonathan Edwards, Jr., distinguished himself. *The Christian Spectator* of January 1822 pointed out the remarkable way in which the career

242 Jonathan and Sarah: An Uncommon Union

of the son paralleled that of the father. After a long pastorate of twenty-seven years in a large church in New Haven, Jonathan Edwards, Jr., was dismissed. He then accepted a post in Colebrook, a frontier town in Connecticut, not far from Stockbridge. He too was invited to become a president, of Union College in Schenectady, only to die a few months after accepting the call at fifty-six.

He was a lesser light, but it shone steadily. As *The Christian Spectator* pointed out, the father possessed an inventive mind. The son was the arranger of facts. The comparison was made of the father to a telescope and the son to a microscope. Both were feared opponents in debate for "The Edwardses would anticipate more objections than the opposer ever dreamed of himself, and then answer them in such a way as to discourage every attempt at reply."

It was said, "It is seldom that a son has such a father, and it is still more rare that such a father leaves behind him a son so worthy of his lineage."

Harriet Beecher Stowe wrote of the Puritans, "They are too honest to dilute the vinegar of life." Such theology produces strong men and strong sons, not too proud to bow the neck to the "frowns of heaven" and to drink "the vinegar of life."